HOW TO
BECOME
A GOOD
CHORAL
SINGER

D1360667

The Choral Singer's Handbook

Roy C. Bennett

Illustrations by DAN MARGULIES

Foreword by ABRAHAM KAPLAN
Director of Choral Music, The Juilliard School

EDWARD B.
MARKS MUSIC
COMPANY /

Exclusive distributor of all printed products:

HAL LEONARD
PUBLISHING
CORPORATION
Winona, MN 55987   Milwaukee, WI 53213

To my dear wife, Ruth, the most understanding of all chorus widows.

Copyright © 1977 by Edward B. Marks Music Company
International Copyright Secured   Made in U.S.A.   All Rights Reserved
Used by permission

Library of Congress Catalog Card No. 75-43350

All rights reserved, including rights of reproduction
and use in any form or by any means, including the
making of copies by any photo process, or by any
electronic or mechanical device, printed, written or
oral, or recording for sound or visual reproduction or for
use in any information storage and retrieval system or
device, unless permission in writing is obtained from
the copyright proprietors.

FOREWORD BY ABRAHAM KAPLAN*

I was struck by one overwhelming feeling while reading the manuscript of this book: the affection which the author holds for his subject, the choral singer.

Another factor which makes these pages unique is that they were written "from the other side of the podium," by someone who has sung in choruses for many years.

There are other books on the various aspects of musical knowledge which go into the training of a good choral singer, but one would be hard-pressed to find a better one than "THE CHORAL SINGER'S HANDBOOK" for anyone in need of the information it offers.

As a choral conductor, I know that my colleagues and I would find our tasks made a good deal easier if our choruses were to read and heed the author's advice.

Abraham Kaplan

---

*Abraham Kaplan is one of the world's foremost choral conductors. He is Director of Choral Music at The Juilliard School in New York City and also founder and conductor of the Camerata Singers.

Contents

AUTHOR'S PREFACE

I'm a choral nut.

I admit it freely, proclaim it joyously, yea, even defiantly. I'll sing it from the housetops, the shower, any forum you name.

I prefer going to my weekly chorus rehearsal to spending the evening playing poker with the boys. I'd rather attend the concert of a good amateur chorus than have the best seat in the house for a star-studded performance at the opera. Time, vocal cords and wife willing, I would sing with choruses every night in the week.

I'm guilty, if trying to promote choral music is a crime. I admit turning conversations with my friends and relatives to my upcoming concerts at any or no provocation. I'm the culprit who bombards them with unsolicited concert mail. I confess to bribing them to buy tickets with promises of free coffee and snacks at my house after the concert.

The not-surprising result of these verbal and postal assaults is that my "victims" invariably thank me for introducing them to the great choral literature.

Multiply me by several hundred thousands, perhaps millions, and you'll have some idea of the number of dedicated choral nuts around the world.

For these beautiful people I wrote this book.

ACKNOWLEDGEMENTS

My deepest gratitude to:

Abraham Kaplan, for believing in me and my book;

George V. Rose, Michael Leavitt, Judith Lang Zaimont and Jack Blumenthal, who read the manuscript and offered many valuable suggestions;

Claire, Neil and Keith, for their enthusiasm and encouragement;

Milton Snitzer, who saw a book in a short list of suggestions for choral singers;

Spencer Tucker, for writing the book proposal that caught the eye of Bernard Kalban, of Edward B. Marks Music Corporation;

And my editor, Ralph Satz, under whose tender loving care the manuscript became a book.

Chapter 1

YOUR CHORUS
SHOPPING GUIDE

"When two Catalans meet, they form a
business partnership; when three get together, they
start a chorus."

Spanish saying

What kinds of singing groups are there for me to choose from? What are their musical requirements? What types of music do they sing?

CHORUS
CHORAL SOCIETY
CHORALE
ORATORIO SOCIETY

Groups whose names contain the above words mainly feature choral works by composers such as Bach, Handel, Mozart, Haydn and Brahms, as well as modern and contemporary composers. Occasionally, some groups may offer operatic choruses, madrigals, spirituals and short novelty choral pieces as a change of pace. Two or three concerts a year may be given.

These are "mixed" groups, made up of both male and female voices, and may range in number from about forty to more than two hundred members. There is usually no age limit, and anyone from senior citizen to junior high school student may join. Singers are drawn from the community. If the group is based in a college, it may include both college students and community members.

Some of these groups require a good knowledge of sightsinging, some require no sightsinging, and most are somewhere in between.

CHOIR

Small singing groups whose primary function is performing liturgical music at services in houses of worship are called choirs. (These amateur groups should not be confused with professional choirs hired by many churches and temples.) Participation may or may not be restricted to members of the congregation. As a rule, no musical knowledge is required and the music is learned by rote. Occasionally a choir may give a concert to raise money.

Inquiries about choirs may be made of your minister or an officer of the congregation. Bulletin boards are a good source of information.

GLEE CLUB

Glee clubs are restricted to either men's or women's voices. Their repertory consists mainly of show tunes, pop tunes, madrigals, folk songs and spirituals. Classical music specially arranged for men's or women's voices is sometimes sung. Glee clubs are generally smaller in membership than choruses. Concerts are given. Usually, no knowledge of sightsinging is required.

INDUSTRIAL CHORUS

Many large corporations sponsor singing groups for their employees. These groups sing Christmas carols, pop tunes, show tunes and an occasional short classical selection. Usually, no sightsinging ability is required.

Find out whether your company has a chorus. If it hasn't, perhaps you can start one.

HIGH SCHOOL CHORUS

In high schools with high musical standards, there is at least one chorus that requires sightsinging ability and one that does not. Everyone sightsings in the "advanced" chorus, while students in the rote group move up to the "advanced" as they learn to read music. Their repertories are mostly classical music.

Some high schools have as many as five singing groups: all-girl, all-boy, a "general" mixed chorus, an "advanced" mixed chorus, and a madrigal group.

In schools where sightsinging is not strictly required, you need only show a desire to sing to become a member of the all-girl, all-boy and "general" mixed chorus. Auditions are held for voice placement, not as a basis for approval or rejection.

In these schools, the "advanced" mixed chorus may consist of all the boys who want to sing, but only the best girls. This is not really an example of male supremacy but a question of numbers. There are always far more girls than boys in high school singing groups and a proper balance of voices dictates the number of singers in each voice section. Unfortunately, this disproportion continues right through to most adult choruses.

The all-girl and all-boy groups usually lean to arrangements of madrigals, pop and show tunes, folk songs and spirituals. The mixed choruses add classical selections.

At least one formal concert a year is given. Groups also perform at assemblies. In addition, a school may have an exchange concert with another school in another city, county or state. There may also be performances at school district choral festivals and state contests. Many schools, whether they require sightsinging or not, put on a "Broadway"-type musical show using a chorus every year.

The best student choral singers are chosen to sing with All-City or All-State choruses, and the best high school choruses often go abroad to give concerts for a few weeks during the summer, if funds are available.

High school singing groups meet from three to five times a week and credit received may be equal to that of a major subject.

COMMUNITY MUSICAL THEATRE GROUPS

Some singing groups, in addition to a regular concert, present a musical production every year.

A good singing voice and acting ability are required for the featured roles. The chorus members need only have a pleasant voice and be able to follow the director's instructions. You don't have to know how to sightsing if you can learn the music quickly.

Auditions are held for featured roles.

Usually, the performers aren't paid, although some of them may have semi-professional experience. They all do it for the fun and love of it, and the performers often show more enthusiasm than their professional counterparts.

BARBERSHOP QUARTETS

Anyone interested in barbershop quartet singing should write to SPEBSQSA (Society for the Preservation and Encouragement of Barbershop Quartet Singing in America) at 6315 Third Avenue, Kenosha, Wisconsin 53141.

For simplification, all the singing groups we have discussed above will be called "choruses" in the following pages.

How Can I Find a Chorus? How Do I Choose the One That's Right for Me?

Most choruses begin rehearsals for their winter concerts immediately after Labor Day, and in December or January for their spring concerts. They then run calls for singers in local newspapers for three or four weeks, starting a week or two before the first rehearsal. Local radio stations with "community bulletin boards" also carry these announcements. Most groups will accept new members during these periods only, because the average choral singer would have great difficulty catching up after missing a number of rehearsals. The exceptions to this rule might be the good sightsinger and the singer who has previously sung the work to be performed at the concert.

However, any time you hear about a chorus you would like to join, don't be fazed. Trot on down and try out—you have nothing to lose.

Choral announcements always include a phone number to call for information. It's a good idea to call before you go. This is what you should find out:

1. *What are their sightsinging requirements?*

The average amateur chorus requires little or no sightsinging ability. They'll welcome you if you can carry a tune and have a pleasant, blending voice. There is a joke among choral singers that choruses will accept anyone who can breathe; men in general and tenors in particular.

Most choruses do not stick rigidly to their requirements. For example, the chorus which asks for "some" sightsinging will rarely turn down a non-sightsinger with a good voice and quick ear. The chorus with high sightsinging standards will almost always accept a fair sightsinger with the above qualifications.

Don't be frightened away by anything you are told when you call. When I was only a fair sightsinger, I was accepted by the chorus with the highest sightsinging requirements in New York City.

2. *What kind of music do they sing? What are the names of the pieces they are rehearsing?*

Ask about music the group sings, so that you can make your choice according to your musical tastes. Ask the names of the works being rehearsed. If you have previously sung in choruses, you may have performed them before and prefer something new. Remember, however, that a work you have already sung can be an altogether different experience with another conductor.

3. *Day, time and length of rehearsal.*

Most choruses meet once a week. Rehearsals usually run between two and three hours. Starting time may be anywhere from 7 to 8:30 P.M. Make sure you have no conflicts on the day of rehearsal. For example, should you have a concert subscription for that night, it would not be fair to the other members of the chorus if you miss rehearsals. As a matter of fact, many choruses will drop you after a given number of unexcused absences.

4. *Directions to the place of rehearsal. Is transportation available?*

Getting directions will also tell you how long it should take you to get there. If time is important to you, add this time to the

length of the rehearsal, plus the time it takes to get home, and see if it fits into your schedule. You may have to find a chorus closer to home. If you don't have transportation, ask if someone in the group lives in your neighborhood and can give you a lift. Choruses will go to great lengths to secure and keep a good member.

5. *What will it cost to join the chorus?*

If you are working on a budget, this is a crucial question. Costs vary greatly among choruses, and some, like college-based groups, may charge nothing at all. Costs can include:

a. *Annual or semi-annual dues.* How much? Can you pay in installments? Is there a special rate for two or more members of the same family? Are "scholarships" available to those who can't afford to pay? Are there special rates for students and senior citizens?

b. *Music.* Does the group supply it or do you have to buy it? If you have to buy it, how much will it cost?

c. *Robes.* If the group wears robes at concerts, do you have to rent one or will the chorus supply one?

d. *Will you have to guarantee a sale of concert tickets?* All groups ask you to sell tickets to their concerts, but some ask you to pay for a certain number of tickets whether you sell them or not.

Before you get the idea that belonging to a singing group is too expensive, measure the cost of one rehearsal (out of approximately thirty rehearsals plus dress rehearsals and concerts) against a night of bowling, bingo or a night at the movies. You'll find it's the greatest entertainment buy in the world!

Choose your group on the basis of your phone calls and go to a rehearsal. If its standards seem a bit above your head, try to join. The best way to improve yourself is to sing with people who are a little better than you are. If they are below your standards, don't join—you will quickly become bored with it.

All singing groups agree that singing is their primary raison d'etre, but differ as to whether it is their function to treat a member as more than just a set of vocal cords.

One new member in a large chorus, by nature a shy person, spent four months in the chorus without ever being spoken to by any of the older members. Left to fend for herself, she and two other new members finally banded together for mutual comfort. She quit after one concert, although the chorus was all she could ask for musically.

Fortunately, there are other groups which, as a matter of policy, go all out to treat new and old members as complete human beings. One such chorus has a "Hospitality" chairperson whose only job it is to make new members feel welcome; its "old" members are urged to introduce themselves to the newcomers; name tags are used to facilitate the introductions; a chatty newsletter and a bulletin board help bring members together; one week after the spring concert, an  annual dinner is held at a local restaurant for members and their families, with entertainment by the members themselves.

All these activities in no way interfere with their serious devotion to music.

A chorus *can* be more than just a singing group!

WHAT TO EXPECT AT YOUR FIRST REHEARSAL

You've made your phone calls and chosen the group that most appeals to you. On the night of the first rehearsal you arrive in good time and—usually, this is what happens next:

The first thing you notice is a group of people milling about, smiling, talking, dressed informally. If it's the first rehearsal after the summer vacation, there are also much handshaking and kissing going on. You may feel left out at the moment, but look at it this way: next year you could be among the kissers and handshakers.

The Table

Drag your eyes away from the happy scene and look around for a table just outside or inside the rehearsal room. There it is! Seated at the table is the group's official greeter, who now takes your name and other pertinent information.

The greeter presents you with a name tag to make it easier for members to say hello and introduce themselves. The names of prospective and regular members are written in different colors. Note your color. If it is red, for example, and you would feel more comfortable tonight talking to kindred and temporarily lonely spirits, look for other people whose names are written in red.

On the table there is a sheet containing information about the group—rules and regulations, dues, rehearsal and concert dates, names of board members, etc. Take one and read it carefully.

Next, you are directed to the music librarian, who lends or sells you the music you will need tonight. If you do not become a member of the group, you can return the music and your money will be refunded.

The Rehearsal Room

You now turn to look at the room in which you may be singing for the next nine months.

Rehearsal rooms come in all sizes and shapes. Some have permanent seats and some do not. If folding chairs are used, members who come early usually unfold and arrange them in rows.

(A note to people with weak backs or other physical ailments that preclude the lifting of chairs, risers, etc.—don't be heroic! If someone asks you to help, tell the truth. I was a hero once and regretted it for months afterwards. Never again! Of course, you can always arrive *after* the chairs have been placed!)

You are told where to sit and the rehearsal begins.

At the end of the rehearsal, the chairs are folded, stacked and put away.

THE REHEARSAL

This is the breakdown of a typical two-hour rehearsal:

Warmup (5–7 minutes)
Work on Music (53–55 minutes)
Intermission (10 minutes)
Work on Music (50 minutes)

The Warmup

The rehearsal starts with a few minutes of vocal warmup. These exercises are intended to help you place your voice correctly and to prepare you to sing with a minimum of strain for the next two hours.

Some conductors do not believe in warmups and plunge right into the music.

Accompaniment is by piano, and how important a good accompanist is!

Work on Music

After the warmup, work on music begins. This is the "meat" of the rehearsal.

In a typical singing group situation, a free and easy relationship exists between the singers and the conductor. You may be surprised to hear the conductor called by his/her first name. Take your cue from the other members. Personally, being rather conservative, I find "first-naming" difficult until I've been a member of a group for a while.

An informal atmosphere makes for a pleasant and enjoyable rehearsal, if it is not overdone. Occasionally, someone may call out a wry comment on the music and the conductor may indulge in a bit of oneupmanship for a laugh. This is fine. It serves to relieve tension and gets one back to the music with renewed seriousness and zest.

But informality sometimes gets out of hand. Chatter can run rampant through the chorus. Or a battle of repartee can develop across the podium. Don't be part of it. It is difficult to accomplish anything in an atmosphere of constant interruption.

Every group has its own ambience and personality. Play it cool until you learn the do's and don'ts of the particular group and then fit into it.

When the music begins, you may at first feel overwhelmed because everyone seems to be sightsinging so well. Remember this: it may be true that some of the people are really doing some darned good sightsinging, but all the others are probably recalling the piece from a previous performance. They probably felt as frustrated when they first sang it as you may feel now.

If you are discouraged after this rehearsal, don't give up. Stay with it. Let this book help you, and you'll overcome those "first-rehearsal blues."

Intermission

After roughly half the scheduled rehearsal time has elapsed, the conductor calls an intermission.

Before everyone disperses, the president of the group welcomes prospective members and makes announcements pertaining to the group. Now you're free to go to the washroom, take a drink of water and a mint, meet new people, or step outside for a smoke (if you must).

The end of the intermission is signalled either by loud chords from the piano, or by the conductor calling "let's go," or by a sergeant-at-arms gently shepherding his strays into the fold.

Work on Music

Work is resumed on the music until the end of the scheduled rehearsal time.

After the rehearsal, the conductor makes some choice comments on the quality of the group's efforts just concluded, tells you which sections of the music to study for the next session and holds auditions for prospective members.

That's what will *usually* happen at your first rehearsal. There are variations on the theme, of course.

A group that holds auditions on a non-rehearsal night, for example, will probably not have an official greeter at the door, only the music iibrarian. The thinking here is that anyone who arrives has passed the audition and is already a full-fledged member. If the group has no hospitality chairperson or committee, it's up to you and the "old" members to get to know one another.

Some groups do not use name tags. Nevertheless, because chorus folk are friendly folk, there will always be someone to come over and make you feel at home.

Chapter 2

IT'S AUDITION TIME!

"You don't have to be a great singer to do great singing."

Robert Shaw

WHAT HAPPENS AT AN AUDITION?

Audition procedures vary according to musical standards. Most of the fine amateur groups in the country hold auditions by appointment on a non-rehearsal night. When you arrive, you are asked to fill out a form that may include questions on your musical training, works previously performed, other organizations you have sung with, etc.

The audition usually takes place with only three people present: the conductor, the accompanist and you. You are asked to do the following:

1. Sing scales.
2. Sing a piece of your own choosing, which you have been asked to bring along with you.
3. Sightsing a passage from music they provide.
4. If necessary, an ear and rhythm test is given, in which you are asked to imitate phrases played on the piano.

You are notified by mail whether you have passed or failed.

Typical amateur community groups are essentially alike in their musical requirements, but may have different audition procedures. Auditions are held on rehearsal nights.

These groups ask only for "some" sightsinging ability, but according to their needs in certain sections may accept non-sightsingers with good voices and ears. The applicant may be asked to fill out a questionnaire, but the headings "musical training," "works performed" and "other organizations" are largely wistful thinking, and blank spaces next to them are the rule rather than the exception.

Auditions may be given by the conductor in the rehearsal room with all the prospective members present or in a separate room privately. Occasionally, the hopefuls are auditioned by a committee of members. Mechanics of the audition are standard: scales to determine your voice category and quality, and sightsinging a few simple measures from the work they are rehearsing. An ear test may also be given.

Applicants may attend several rehearsals before auditioning. Acceptances and rejections are by mail, but the lucky ones are often given the good news surreptitiously by the conductor or a Good Samaritan in the know.

How Can I Prepare Myself
for a Successful Audition?

It's only natural to be nervous. Many of the world's great artists admit to having "butterflies" before every performance. Let this console you—nervous people make better and more sensitive interpreters of music than phlegmatic types.

The following hints should decrease the rate of your heartbeat and increase your chances of being accepted.

The chorus needs you. They are as anxious for you to succeed as you are. Why else would they advertise for members?

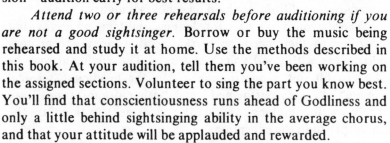

The people who do the auditioning are on your side. Whether it's the conductor or a committee of chorus members, they've all been in your shoes before and understand what you're going through. They will do their best to put you at ease and help you in every way to make your audition a successful one.

Audition early. On the night you audition, volunteer to be first. At least, be among the first. Waiting only increases tension—audition early for best results.

Attend two or three rehearsals before auditioning if you are not a good sightsinger. Borrow or buy the music being rehearsed and study it at home. Use the methods described in this book. At your audition, tell them you've been working on the assigned sections. Volunteer to sing the part you know best. You'll find that conscientiousness runs ahead of Godliness and only a little behind sightsinging ability in the average chorus, and that your attitude will be applauded and rewarded.

Before auditioning, make a good impression at rehearsals. You must look at the conductor, who is continually scanning the group, at all times. Keeping your head buried in the music is a cardinal sin, and if you do it you are sure to be noticed.

In borderline cases, the members who sit next to you may be consulted as to your personal traits. Do you engage in distracting non-essential conversation during rehearsal? Are you amenable to corrections? All in all, would you be an asset to the chorus?

It's safe to say that anyone who has a pleasant voice and can carry a tune will find a home in some singing group somewhere.

Chapter 3

YOU'RE IN THE CHORUS NOW!

> ".... each musician must learn to play, on the one hand, as if he were a soloist, and on the other, with the constant awareness of being an indispensable part of a team. It is this quality of human teamwork—the sense of being one of a group working together to achieve the ultimate in beauty—that has always afforded me a joy . . . that no solo performance can duplicate.
>
> "We share a great privilege . . . the privilege of bringing masterpieces to life. We also share a sacred responsibility. We are entrusted with the duty of interpreting these masterpieces with utter integrity."

> *Pablo Casals*

Excerpt from JOYS and SORROWS, Reflections by Pablo Casals, as told to Albert E. Kahn, © 1970 by Albert E. Kahn, published by Simon & Schuster, Inc., United States and Canada; for the United Kingdom and British Commonwealth, excluding Canada: Macdonald and Jane's Publishers. Used by permission.

WHAT TO DO AT HOME

Can I Become a Good Choral Singer if I'm Not a Good Sightsinger?

Yes. Some of the most reliable choral singers are only fair readers who conscientiously rehearse their music at home. Daily rehearsals, if only for a few minutes, are best. After dinner, instead of watching a rerun movie on TV, rerun your music.

Knowing your part will give you confidence and add immeasurably to your enjoyment of rehearsals and concerts.

Instead of being a leaner on the person next to you, become a "leanee."

TRICKS OF THE TRADE

I'm Conscientious, Still I Have Trouble Learning My Part. Are There Any Short Cuts or "Tricks of the Trade" that Can Help?

There are many "tricks," mostly common sense, used by the best choral singers, that can show you

- how to make your part stand out on the page;
- how to find your entrance note;
- how to learn your notes in groups rather than singly;
- how to count;
- how to mark intervals, degrees of the scale, accented and unaccented notes, and pronunciations;
- how to know the first note on the next page before you turn the page;
- how to avoid singing wrong words or syllables with your music;
- how to count beats so the audience can't tell;
- how to avoid many other mistakes that amateur choral singers are apt to make;
- how to hold your music and turn pages quietly.

Let's look at some examples.

(All the markings in this section are of my devising. Markings are a very personal thing, however. Don't hesitate to use your own if they make better sense to you.)

How To Make Your Part Stand Out on the Page

"Paint" Your Part

With four and sometimes eight voice parts on a page, things can get mighty confusing.

As soon as you get your music home, "paint" (highlight) your part with a broad tip permanent type yellow marker. Carter's "Highliter" and "Major Accent" are excellent for this purpose.

Highlighting will make it easier for you to follow your part and will prevent you from reading another line by mistake. It's also a good idea to own a copy of everything you sing. You can then mark it up any way you choose and have it available with your own markings for future performances.

How to Find Your Entrance Note.

Finding your entrance note is half the battle of sight-singing. Many amateur choral singers wait for their neighbors to sing the note first, then sing it themselves a split second later. This is undoubtedly the shortest split second known to man, imperceptible to both audience and conductor.

But there is danger in relying on someone else. What if your neighbor doesn't know the note, either? Or enters at the wrong time? Or not at all? Or is absent?

There is a great feeling of competence and satisfaction in knowing the pitch of the entrance note and exactly when to enter. It's a feeling you will experience if you faithfully practice the following techniques.

"Steal" Your Note

Most of you reading that sub-title may have been a little taken aback: "I, steal?" One or two of you may not have been fazed in the least.

Choruses are made up of people from all walks of life, and it is possible that among them there may be an occasional horsethief.

Rest assured that "stealing" is perfectly legal and even encouraged in choral singing.

"Stealing" is possible because your entrance note is almost always sounded in another part before you have to sing it. It may be in one of the other three choral parts, the solo part or the accompaniment. It may even be in your own part.

How do you "steal" a note?

At home, if you know the names of the notes, study the score without listening to the music and try to find your entrance note in another part. (If you can't read music, see Page 39 on the use of the record player and the tape recorder.) Once you have found the note you need, mark in #2 pencil as indicated in the examples below.

Let the other voice parts do as much of your work for you as possible.

"Stealing" Your Entrance Note from Another Part

Problem:

In this example, you (the alto) have to find your entrance note (third measure, second beat, F♯).

Fig. 1

"*Gloria*," *Vivaldi*

Solution:

In looking over the music, you see that the soprano sings the F♯ just one beat before you do.

In pencil, instruct yourself to listen to the sopranos by drawing an arrow to the soprano part. Then circle the F♯ in the soprano part, draw a line to your part, and circle the F♯ in your part.

To be even more specific, you may write "follow soprano" in your part.

At rehearsal, you simply heed your own instructions and listen to the sopranos when that point in the music is reached.

A very helpful technique is that of humming the soprano line softly in your range as the sopranos sing. Don't hum too loudly or you'll disturb your neighbors.

If this particular "steal" does not work for you, erase your pencil markings at home and try to find another.

"Stealing" Your Entrance Note from the Accompaniment

Problem:

You are a bass looking for your entrance note (first measure, third beat, D).

 Fig. 2

"Ah, the Thought Which Torments Me," Marenzio, © Marks Music Corporation

Solution:

Examining the music, you discover that the D is sounded in the accompaniment in the first two beats of the measure.

Hum the D as it is being played, until your entrance. Mark as indicated.

"Stealing" Your Note from Your Own Part

Problem:

Here you have just sung an A, and after a three beat rest, must enter again on an A.

Fig. 3

"Missa Iste Confessor," Palestrina © Marks Music Corporation

Solution:

After you have sung the first A, hum it softly for three beats and sing A again on your entrance.

In humming, be careful to hold on to the correct pitch, especially if the other parts contain a note that clashes with it.

Mark as indicated.

To help you count, you can write in the number of beats of rest from one A to the other.

"Stealing" Your Note Stepwise from Another Part

You can't always expect to find your exact entrance note sounded before you come in. But sometimes another part will lead you into it.

Problem:

In this example, the basses must enter on an F (second measure, third beat).

Fig. 4

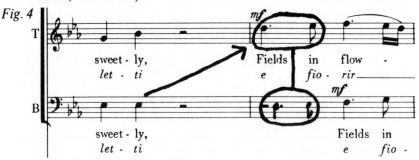

"Ah, Weary Am I," Marenzio © Marks Music Corporation

Solution:

You find that the tenors lead into your part stepwise (D, E♭, F).

Indicate that you are to follow the tenor part by drawing the appropriate arrow.

Circle the lead-in notes and write them into your part in your range. Draw a line connecting the tenor part to your part.

At rehearsal, follow the tenors and hum the lead-in notes softly in your range as the tenors sing them. They will lead you beautifully into your note.

You can also find your entrance note stepwise from your part in this example. Simply hum for four beats the E♭ you've just sung, then enter one step higher, on the F.

Now suppose you are the soprano in the following example. Your entrance note is first measure, fourth beat, F♯. (The key is G).

Fig. 5

"Requiem," Brahms

"Steal" your note from the soloist. Simply hum the F♯ and E as the soloist sings them and then go back to the F♯. Mark as indicated.

(Since soloists usually don't appear until the dress rehearsal, you may have to find a second best "steal" till then.)

"Stealing" Your Entrance Note by Thinking Back

Problem:

Your entrance note in the second measure is B, but alas, the last note you've sung is an F♯, which is a long way from B.

Fig. 6

lu - jah,   HUM   King   of

Solution:

Fortunately, the note you sang before the F♯ is a B, exactly the note you want.

Sing the B and F♯, then immediately think back to the B. Hum the B softly, count and hold until your entrance.

How to Learn Notes in Groups Rather than Singly.

Always look for the opportunity to learn your notes by the fistful rather than one at a time. You'll discover that you can conquer pages at an unbelievable rate.

In the following examples, your ear is the predominant tool.

Phrases

A phrase is a section of a musical line, rather like a clause or a sentence in prose.

Sometimes a whole phrase is sung in another part before it is sung in yours.

Fig. 7   Lively

I   1. It was on one Sun-day   morn-ing   Sun-day

II   1. It was   on   one Sun-day

"Six Afro-American Carols for Easter." Clark © Marks Music Corporation

In this example, you can learn five notes at one time just by listening to and imitating another voice part.

Mark as indicated.

Two Measures for the Price of One

You can learn two measures by learning only one if they are musically identical. The trick is to recognize that they are identical and mark them accordingly.

Fig. 8

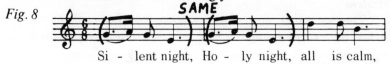

Si - lent night, Ho - ly night, all   is calm,

Put each of the two measures in parentheses and write "SAME" between them.

Scales

A scale is a group of notes arranged in a prescribed order, usually in whole and half steps. (For a more detailed explanation, see Page 69.)

Some consecutive notes you will come across in your music are scales or parts of scales, ascending (going up) or descending (going down).

Fig. 9

Joy   to the world, the Lord   is   come,   –

This is an example of a complete major scale descending.

Put parentheses around the scale and circle the degree numbers over each note if necessary. Also indicate whether it is a major or a minor scale.

Chords

A chord is a group of at least three notes, usually arranged in thirds. (A detailed explanation of chords starts on Page 105.)

You can learn three or more notes at a time if you know the sound of chords, recognize them and mark them on your copy.

Write the appropriate numbers over the notes of the chords and circle: (1) , (3) , (5) , (♭7) , (8) . Write "CHORD" or name of chord if you know it.

Fig. 10

Ich   will euch trö –   –   sten

"Requiem," Brahms

Sequences

Sequences are phrases repeated higher or lower in pitch. They will frequently appear in your music. By learning the phrase and using your ear, you can learn several measures at a time.

Put the sequences in parentheses and mark "SEQ."

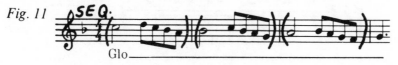

Fig. 11

Sections Repeated

Sections of words and music are sometimes repeated. One example is a part of the "Hosanna" from Mozart's "Mass in C Minor."

Once you recognize the repeat, simply mark "REPEAT" and be grateful to Wolfgang Amadeus for a few pages you don't have to learn.

A section is sometimes repeated with different words. In the Mozart "Requiem," the "Lux aeterna" and "cum sanctis" parts of the final section are musically almost identical with the "Exaudi" and "Kyrie eleison" parts of the "Requiem" section, but the words are different.

There are some musical differences. Be aware of them and pencil them in to avoid wrong notes.

A Phrase that Sounds like Something Else

If a phrase sounds like something from another work or song, note this.

For example, in Leonard Bernstein's "Chichester Psalms," there is a phrase in the bass part that is exactly the melody of "by the dawn's early light" from "The Star Spangled Banner."

In his music, one bass wrote above the Hebrew; "by the dawn's early light." You may think it's funny, but he had the last laugh by learning six notes at one time—and that's almost like winning the blue ribbon at a cake bake or hitting a grand slam home-run.

Fig. 12

"Chichester Psalms," Bernstein © Amberson Enterprises, Inc. Used by Permission.

General Hints

Counting

Help yourself count by numbering the beats in the bar, if necessary.

Fig. 13

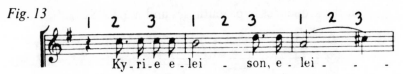

"*Mass in G,*" *Schubert* ® *Marks Music Corporation.*

Complicated Measures

Measures that look rhythmically complicated become simple when you divide them into beats by vertical lines.

Fig. 14

"*Mass,*" *Dello Joio* ® *Marks Music Corporation.*

Holding Notes

Remind yourself to hold a note to its full value by drawing an arrow to the point of release.

Fig. 15

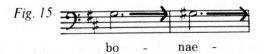

Syncopated Notes

Bars containing notes that start on normally unaccented beats or parts of beats (syncopation) can be read more easily when you divide each beat into halves, downbeat (↓) and upbeat (↑), and mark. For a further explanation of the arrows, see Page 57.

In this example, the arrows clearly show that only the first note is sung on the downbeat, while all the others start on the upbeat.

Fig. 15a

The picture becomes even clearer if you break down the quarter notes into eighth notes, mark and add vertical lines separating the bar into beats.

Fig. 15 a

la la   la   la   la

Final Consonants

Count the number of beats over a long-held note and write in the final consonant when it should be pronounced.

Fig. 16

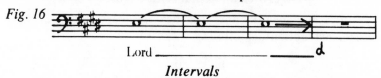

Lord _____ ___ d

Intervals

Intervals are marked with the abbreviation of the interval between the two notes, over a line connecting the notes: e.g., "8" for octave, "m3" for minor third, etc. (See Table of Intervals, Page 88.)

Fig. 17

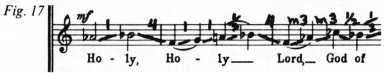

Ho - ly,   Ho - ly___   Lord,___ God of

"Mass," Dello Joio © Marks Music Corporation.

If the interval is larger than an octave, think an octave higher, mark the octave, then reckon the interval from the octave.

Mark as indicated.

Fig. 18

wer - - den.   Die___

"Requiem," Brahms

Repeated Leaps from the Same Note

This example can be read in two ways:

First, by interval:

Fig. 18a

Second and more simply:

Regard the repeated "g"s as one line. Play, sing and remember. Regard the "d, c, b" as a separate line. Play, sing and remember.

Putting it together:

After singing the first "g" and finding the "d" by the Interval Method (Page 88), repeat the "g"s from memory and the "c, b" from memory or read by the Interval Method.

Mark as below.

Fig. 18b

Accented and Unaccented Notes

Mark in accented and unaccented notes per your conductor's instructions as follows:

              ╱ : accented

              ‿ : unaccented

Fig. 19

"Requiem," Brahms

Last Note on a Page or Staff

After the last note on each page, extend the staff lines and write in the first note and word of the next page, especially before a page turn. In fast music, this is useful even in the middle of a page. *Never be caught by surprise.*

Fig. 20

Wrong Words

If you're singing wrong words or syllables with your notes, circle both the notes and the text under it.

Fig. 21

First and Second Endings

First and second ending symbols ‖1.   ‖2.
are usually printed only over the soprano part. Draw them heavily over your own part.

Repeat Marks
Darken and enlarge repeat marks.

Fig. 22

"Don't Move"

Where the accompaniment continues after the chorus has finished singing, write "DON'T MOVE." Then don't move or put down your music until the instrumental portion is completed.

Fig. 23

"*Requiem,*" *Brahms*

Direction of Notes

Where two consecutive notes are only one step or a half step apart, the eye may see them as the same pitch. Conversely, where notes are of the same pitch, the eye may see them as different pitches.

Draw lines between the notes showing the direction of movement. A horizontal line denotes same pitch.

Fig. 24

Enharmonic Changes

Where two consecutive notes are of the same pitch but spelled differently, mark to avoid singing two different pitches.

Fig. 25

Two Lines of Text

Often the text is given in two languages. (See Fig. 25.) Pencil out the language not being used to avoid confusion.

Two Vocal Lines on One Staff

In music where two vocal lines are printed on one staff, confusion often arises when the notes of the upper line fall below the notes of the lower line or when the bar looks cluttered.

Pencil out the notes (and words) not in your part, so that only your notes (and words) are clearly visible. If you own the music, use black ink.

Fig. 25a   Fig. 25b   Har - ri-gan, that's

Em-per-or, Czar, or a

© George M. Cohan Music Corp.

Pronunciation

If a syllable or word is not pronounced the way it looks, mark it in. Don't mispronounce it week after week.

Fig. 26

Gra - ~~si~~ - as

tsi

Dynamic Markings

Darken, enlarge and circle dynamic markings for greater legibility.

Sudden Change of Tempo

Before a sudden change of tempo, warn yourself by writing "faster" or "slower" just before the change.

Counting Covertly

You can count beats by tapping your big toe inside your shoes or by pressing your fingers against the score. Never move your lips when you count, or tap your foot: it is unprofessional and will distract your audience.

Doubled Parts

Basses will often find their parts doubled in the orchestral part (piano part in rehearsal). Listen for it.

When the bass "lays out" (has no notes to sing), the tenor part may be featured in the pia~ .

In music for women's voices, the alto part may be doubled by the piano.

Think about how you can make music reading easier for yourself. Any mark may be used, even though it may not make sense to anyone else. If it works for you, that's all that counts.

By Now, My Music Looks Like a Road Map. Is that Good or Bad?

A good choral singer marks up his copy. Professionals do it too.

Conversely, you can almost always tell a poor choral singer by the absence of markings on his copy.

Have You Marked Your Copy?

Fig. 27

A Page from the Author's Copy of Brahms' "Requiem"

© G. Schirmer, Inc. Used by Permission.

13748

(The author on his copy has used a yellow marker to distinguish his bass part.)

How to Hold Your Music

When a chorus is rehearsing "Lift Thine Eyes" from Mendelssohn's "Elijah," it is a rare conductor who can resist the temptation to say: "I wish you would lift thine eyes and look at me!"

You and your fellow singers are vocal instruments used by the conductor to express his interpretation of the music. Each voice line should be sung with the precision and musicianship of a fine orchestral section. This is impossible to achieve unless every member of the chorus watches the conductor. But not everyone does.

Some people, "just too tired" after "a hard day at the office" or "in the kitchen," bury the music and their heads in their laps.

Others, with the best of intentions, try to look at the conductor but lose their places after taking their eyes away from the music.

If you want to watch the conductor and find it difficult, chances are that these two factors are the cause of your trouble:

1. Excessive movement of your eyes from the music to the conductor.
2. Excessive movement of your head from the music to the conductor.

In the position I recommend for holding the music, the first factor is minimized and the second completely eliminated.

First, let's see what happens when you hold your music incorrectly.

Position 1 (the worst): the music is in your lap.

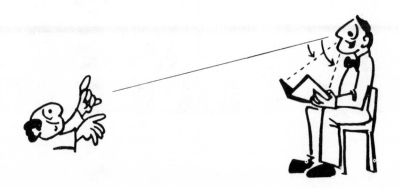

Note how far your eye has to move from the page to the conductor. The angle is steep from the top of the page, and even worse when you reach the bottom of the page.

With the music in your lap, it is impossible for you to look at the conductor without bobbing your head. Small wonder you can lose your place when the music is in this position.

Position 2 (the most commonly used): the music is held up in an almost vertical position so that the top of the page appears to be just under the conductor's hands.

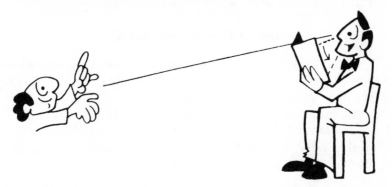

The angles in this position are much better than those in position 1. You may even be able to see both the conductor and the top of the page at the same time.

From the bottom of the page, however, the angle is still steep. Your eye must travel all the way up and over the top of the page to see the conductor, then back again. Head-bobbing is still involved and you can still lose your place.

Position 3 (recommended as the best): the music is held up almost horizontally, sufficiently away from you so that you can see the conductor even from the bottom of the page.

Note how small the top and bottom angles are in this position as compared with Positions 1 and 2.

Now you can look at the music and see the conductor peripherally at the same time. If you want to look at the conductor only, it requires a very small movement of your eyes. No head-bobbing is involved. You are much less likely to lose your place when you return to the music.

It may be necessary for you to wear bifocals or half glasses to see both the conductor and the music clearly. Call these your "chorus" glasses and get a pair—they're a good investment.

How to Turn Pages Quietly

In choral music, flipping a page noisily can ruin a mood at a concert just as surely as a cough, a sneeze or a child's cry. Pages must be turned quietly, particularly in soft passages.

An ingenious system of preparing pages for turning has been developed by Flora Horowitz of the Great Neck (N.Y.) Choral Society. It is by far the best one I've seen, and I'm delighted to pass it along to you (with one small variation of my own).

With a pair of scissors, cut a triangular corner from the bottom of the first right-hand page. It should be large enough to accommodate the tip of your right thumb.

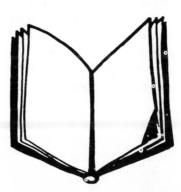

Along the bottom edge of the following right-hand page, cut a triangular wedge large enough to accommodate the tip of your right thumb. Make sure this cut is an inch or two to the left of the corner cut on the previous page.

Alternate corner and inside cuts throughout your music. (Flora cuts the corners and *outside* edges of alternating pages. If this is more comfortable for you, do it her way.)

Cut only pages with chorus parts. Use paper clips on solo and long instrumental sections, staggering the clips along the top of your copy.

Now that the pages are prepared, let's go on to the actual turning process.

Step 1 (basic holding position): Hold the music at the bottom with both hands, one under the left-hand pages and the other under the right-hand pages, with your thumbs on top. (With very heavy copies, when most of the pages you are holding are still on the right-hand side, the fingers of the left hand may have to be turned diagonally over the binding to help support the right hand.)

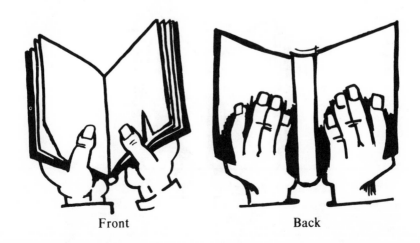

Front   Back

Step 2: (To be done well in advance of the page turn.) Move the tip of your thumb to where the page has been cut, so that you are touching the page underneath. Bend the right-hand pages with your thumb and right-hand fingers and slip your thumb under the page to be turned.

Step 2

Step 3: Shift back to the basic holding position, except for your right thumb in its new position.

Step 3

Step 4: At the page turn, bring both hands together as if you were closing the music and lift your left thumb out of the way. The page you are turning will join the left hand pages.

Step 5: Open the music and hold as in Step 1. Go to Step 2 as soon as practicable in preparation for the next page turn.

Step 4   Step 5

Practice this method of page turning at home. You'll find it fast, efficient and virtually silent.

Summary: *What to Do the First Week You Have Your Music Home:*

1. "Paint" your part with a yellow marker.
2. Cut wedges for turning.
3. Mark your copy as indicated in this chapter.
4. Use paper clips on solo and long instrumental parts.
5. Write your name, address, phone number, rehearsal and concert information conspicuously on your copy.

What is the Best Way to Learn My Part at Home?

Imagine that you are a dedicated choral singer who rehearses the Vivaldi "Gloria" with a chorus about two hours a week.

Progress is slow and the conductor beseeches you and your fellow members to do better. You would dearly love to comply, but you can't read music at all, or at best, very little. What to do?

You've thought of a solution to your problem, but alas, it is impossible to achieve . . . your chorus neighbor on the right, that pillar you lean on, that genius who sightsings the "Gloria's" most difficult passages; if you could only take that neighbor home with you for a week until the next rehearsal . . . Oh, well. There must be another way, you sigh.

There is another way.

Meanwhile, your more musically knowledgeable neighbors find the task of sitting down at the piano and picking out their parts a chore and a bore.

There is another way for them, too.

The solution lies in the use of modern electronics: a high fidelity system that includes a record player and/or a tape recorder.

Playing a recording of the "Gloria" is almost like having the chorus at home with you. You can rehearse at your convenience, repeat difficult passages, correct your mistakes, avoid baleful glances from your conductor, etc.

Although many choral singers learn their parts without a record player and tape recorder, it can be done much more efficiently, enjoyably and quickly with them. If you don't own a hi-fi setup and you really want to become a good choral singer in a hurry, get one and use it as described later. It can change you from a pebble to the Rock of Gibraltar.

Whether or not you own hi-fi equipment, you should have a musical instrument at home so that you can play your part once you've learned to read music. If you can't spend too much money, a 12-tone toy piano or xylophone will do. There are also some moderately priced instruments available, such as the two-octave Suzuki Melodion and the Hohner Melodia. These are wind instruments with keyboards. By far the best buy for your purpose is one of the surprisingly inexpensive three-octave electric organs on the market (Magnus, Estey, etc.)

I Don't Read Music at All, and I Don't Own a Hi-fi System. How Can I Learn My Part?

People with good musical ears can do quite well even if they have not yet learned how to sightsing. Here are some of the things that will help you learn your part:

Have someone mark your copy as suggested in the section on "Tricks of the Trade." The markings will make more and more sense to you as you study this book.

Between rehearsals, go over your part with someone who knows it or can play it for you.

Own a hi-fi system!

Introducing SARA—a little lady who will help you become a good choral singer:

Study this book.

Attend rehearsals regularly.

Rehearse daily if possible.

Attend part rehearsals. Groups often have extra rehearsals for each voice section. Take advantage of these sessions.

I Now Read Music a Little. What Do I Do?

At home, look over your music, and if it hasn't yet been done, mark as suggested in the section on "Tricks of the Trade."

Try to learn your part a phrase at a time by playing it on your instrument and singing it. Play and sing each phrase until you learn it.

SARA, of course!

When are you going to buy that hi-fi system?

Just Went Out and Bought a Hi-fi—How Do I Use It to Help Me Learn My Part? This Had Better Be Good!

OK, you won't be sorry.

First: If You Have a Record Player Only.

Buy or borrow a recording of the work you are studying. Your public library may have it. While you are playing it, listen for your part and try to sing along. Repeat phrases as often as necessary until you learn them.

At first you may have trouble distinguishing your part from everything else that's going on in the recording. On records, compositions written for chorus and orchestra too often turn out to be showpieces for the orchestra with a muddy chorus lurking somewhere in the background. Choral concerts often sound that way too. Why this should be so is one of music's great mysteries.

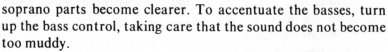

Fortunately, modern electronic wizardry can improve this unfavorable voice-to-instrument balance.

By turning up (increasing gain on) your treble control, soprano parts become clearer. To accentuate the basses, turn up the bass control, taking care that the sound does not become too muddy.

Increase the gain on a mid-range control to bring out the entire chorus in relation to the orchestra. All vocal notes over 250 Hz are made more audible (middle C is 256 Hz.) This includes almost all of the soprano, most of the alto, nearly half of the tenor, and the upper bass range.

On stereo systems, use your balance control to see whether favoring one channel over the other will make your part more distinguishable.

The combination of your chorus rehearsals, extra sessions and any assistance you get at home will also help you pick your notes out of the recording.

Incidentally, the better your hi-fi equipment, the easier it will be for you to hear your part.

Using a record player alone is rather cumbersome because it is difficult to find the exact groove on the record when you want to repeat a passage or find a particular section.

Second: If You Have a Tape Recorder Only.

The procedure is the same as using a record player, except that the tape counter (if you have one on your machine) will make it easier for you to find your place. (See use of tape counter below.)

The trouble with using tape alone is that the tape repertory of classical music is limited. Even if you should find a tape of the work you are rehearsing, you will have to "fast forward" your way through solos and long instrumental passages every time you rehearse.

The third method, which uses both a record player and a tape recorder, is by far the best.

Third: If You Have a Record Player and a Tape Recorder (Reel-to-Reel, Cassette or Cartridge).*

Buy or borrow a recording of the work you are studying.

Set the tape counter to 000. (A tape recorder with a "memory" rewind is preferable.)

Tape the choral sections of the work from the recording. Omit long solos and instrumental passages. This will save you much rehearsal time.

Write the counter number that begins each section on your music. For example, in the Mozart "Requiem": 000—"Requiem"; 231—"Dies Irae"; 460—"Rex Tremendae"; etc.

Now if you are looking for the "Dies Irae," you can easily and precisely find it by winding your tape to 231.

A difficult passage at 239? No problem. Rewind the tape to 239 and play it again. And again. And again. You'll learn it in minutes.

If you are having trouble distinguishing your part, pick out the notes on your instrument and then listen again to the tape. Repeat until you don't need the instrument any more.

If your finances permit, buy rather than borrow records.

"A record library," to parody John Keats, "is a joy forever: its loveliness increases; it will never pass into nothingness."

Don't be afraid that the recording you buy to learn your part will become dusty on your shelf. You'll play it again and again, thrilling to the great music and enjoying the memories of the one, unique concert it invokes.

Imagine reliving a highlight of your life at will!

WARNING: The use of a tape recorder to copy a recording was illegal at the time of publication of this book. This procedure is described for your use only in the event it becomes legal in the future. As of January 1978 a new federal copyright law encompassing what is "fair use" may be consulted to avoid illegal usage of duplicating equipment.

Which Recording Should I Buy of the Work We're Rehearsing?

Schwann's Catalogs 1 and 2, a complete listing of currently available records and tapes, offer you a bewildering variety of choices.

In my list of "RECOMMENDED RECORDINGS OF POPULAR CHORAL WORKS" on Page 124, I have chosen two recordings of each work (wherever possible)—one "budget"-priced and one standard-priced. The inexpensive recording is adequate as a learning tool, but you may prefer to buy "the best."

If you are economy-minded, look for records that offer two popular choral works. Take advantage of record sales in your area.

Seraphim, Odyssey, Heliodor and RCA Victrola offer at bargain prices recordings that were formerly issued under the Angel, Columbia, Deutsche Grammophon and RCA Victor labels respectively. They are excellent buys.

A stereo record is not necessarily better than a mono. It's the performance that counts.

See the Schwann catalogs wherever records are sold for a listing of available versions of any given work.

Schwann's also lists available records of musical shows. The original cast album is musically most like the version performed by your community theatre group.

As far as folk songs, spirituals and barbershop arrangements are concerned, there are so many arrangements of these songs that you will probably not find the one you're working on recorded.

At the back of the book I've also included a list of record review publications. You can keep up to date on the latest records and what the experts think of them by consulting these publications. Look for them in the music reference section of your public library.

WHAT TO DO AT REHEARSAL

How Can I Do Well at Rehearsals?

Arrive a few minutes early and get settled.

Bring a pencil and use it lavishly. A good choral singer is never without one.

Don't trust your memory from one rehearsal to the next, but immediately write down the conductor's instructions: dynamics, tempos, pronunciations, etc. Give yourself every break to make your job easier.

Sing with your ears. Listen to the other parts while you are singing your own.

Be more concerned with the total effect of the group than with your own voice.

Put a "?" wherever you are having difficulty, then particularly practice those spots at home.

If you are confused, ask the conductor for clarification. Be concise in your questions. Go from the general to the specific. Slowly name the page, brace (score, system), voice part, measure and beat in that order. For example: "page twelve, middle brace, soprano line, third measure, second beat."

Pay attention to the conductor at all times, even when he is working on parts other than your own.

If you are not sure of notes, don't sing. Imagine someone singing wrong notes with authority!

If you are lost, don't try to catch up by repeating notes the chorus has already sung. Come in again precisely where the chorus is singing.

Learn to look at the conductor while reading your music. This can be accomplished only by holding the music up, so that you can see both at the same time. If you wear glasses, you may need bifocals or half glasses to see both clearly. If we all sang with our heads in the music, metronomes would replace conductors.

At home, after you know your part fairly well, simulate rehearsal conditions by holding the music up and looking away from it periodically.

Where the conductor *particularly* wants you to watch him for a special effect, write "WATCH" or draw ∽

If your neighbor repeatedly makes the same mistake, say: "We seem to disagree on this note. Am I wrong?" *You* may very well turn out to be the culprit!

Write instructions pertaining to choral activities in pencil conspicuously on your copy of the music: sections to be rehearsed for the following week; dates, times and places of rehearsals and concerts; a number assigned to you; etc. Inside and outside covers are the best places.

Turn pages quietly. Paper clips should be used when skipping several pages.

Here's one you may have heard before: SARA!

Call the designated person if you cannot attend a rehearsal.

After the rehearsal has begun, save your socializing and repartee for the intermission. Listen to the conductor and limit your talking to essentials. Discourage your neighbor from talking to you. Many a good choral singer cancels his/her value to the chorus by creating distractions.

Take the allotted time for intermission and do not straggle in late.

As a chorus member, be especially careful of your personal hygiene. Singing in a group means close physical contact with your neighbors and nothing will turn them off faster than body odor, bad breath, onions and garlic. If possible, shower before each rehearsal and put on fresh clothing. If you don't have time to shower, a wash, deodorant and, if possible, a change of clothes should do the trick.

Singing for an hour dries the mouth. During the intermission, a refreshing drink of water and a mint are in order. Use "Sen-Sen," "Tic-Tac," or a small hard candy, but nothing that will last into the start of the second half of the rehearsal. Some choruses supply a dish of mints gratis for members.

WHAT TO DO AT THE CONCERT

What Can I Do to Make the Concert a Success?

Eat lightly and not too close to concert time.

If naps tend to make you sluggish, don't.

A shower, ending with a dash of cold water, should help.

Arrive at the concert hall in plenty of time to do whatever you have to do and relax.

Bring your music. (And robe and glasses, if any.)

"Every public appearance carries with it a definite responsibility in stage deportment," says the American Academy of Teachers of Singing.

Make sure your robe (or dress or suit) is cleaned and pressed.

Dress in the designated manner. The ladies are usually asked not to wear earrings or jewelry that may flash and distract the audience.

Respect yourself and your audience will respect you. Coming on stage, walk erect and look straight ahead. Don't talk, laugh, or wave at friends or relatives.

Make sure you stop squarely in front of your seat so that none is skipped.

On signal, sit down in unison with the rest of the chorus. Touching elbows with your neighbors helps. Nothing looks more amateurish than sloppy sitting and rising.

Sit down and stand up as quietly as possible.

On sitting down after singing, always feel for your chair. You may have moved away from it.

If you are seated on the highest riser and there is danger of falling over backwards, constantly check the position of your chair.

When you are seated, be quiet.

Watch the Conductor!

Once you begin to sing, find a comfortable position so that you can see both your music and the conductor with a minimum of fidgeting.

If you sing a wrong note, don't call attention to it by placing your hand over your mouth or grimacing.

Don't keep your head in the music. By concert time the music should pretty well be in your head, anyway.

Avoid singing mannerisms that distract the audience: obvious time-beating, excessive movement of the head or body, smiling at someone in the audience, etc. (Ask your friends and relatives to tell you honestly whether you have such mannerisms. If you have, correct them for the next concert.)

Face the conductor, not the audience. This is especially important if you are at or near the ends of the stage. Both feet should be in a straight line with the conductor.

During the performance, don't let your mind wander. Pay attention to every mark you've made in your copy.

Concentrate, concentrate, concentrate!—until the last note is sung and the last chord sounded. Then bask in the applause of a job well done.

Leave the stage in a professional manner.

Other Chorus Activities

How Can I Help the Chorus Other than by Singing?

Working for the chorus can be a very rewarding experience. You may have a talent your group can use. Your board of directors includes people in charge of accounting, legal matters, publicity, fund-raising, membership, ticket sales, the music library, etc.

Pay your dues promptly. The chorus has monetary obligations such as paying the salaries of the conductor, the accompanist, and many other expenses incidental to running a chorus.

Your board of directors will be happy to have you attend one of its meetings. Go—you'll be amazed and fascinated by the amount of work that goes on behind the scenes. The coffee and cake served afterwards are delicious, too. It's a great opportunity to collect some marvelous new recipes.

Go out of your way to be friendly to other members of the chorus, especially the new ones. A warm and relaxed atmosphere leads to better singing and a smaller turnover in membership.

You can also render valuable service by selling tickets to your concert (you are actually doing people a favor by introducing them to the great choral literature); by composing and typing letters and notices; by addressing and stuffing envelopes; by designing and distributing posters; by asking business firms and private individuals to be sponsors; by finding worthy new members; by helping with robes at concert time; by folding and stacking chairs at rehearsals, if necessary; by editing a newsletter; etc.

Form small groups to sing in hospitals, libraries, schools, etc. You will be doing a good deed and promoting better community relations at the same time.

If you know your part, volunteer to help others in your voice section to learn theirs at special rehearsals.

If you volunteer to do only one job for the chorus during the year, it will be a great help to your hard-working board of directors.

How Can I Keep in Good Choral Shape between Seasons?

Over the summer, that dull and interminable season between choral rehearsals, you can get a good head start by studying the music the chorus will be performing at the winter concert.

Find out from your conductor the pieces you will be singing, the editions he will use, and the sections to be omitted (if any). Get the music, study it, and amaze your choral neighbors at the first rehearsal in September.

Some choruses run "sings" during the summer. For a small entrance fee, a chorus will provide a conductor, accompanist, soloists and copies of the music to be sung.

The program may consist of one long work or several shorter works. Sometimes, for example, the entire evening is devoted to the Bach "B minor Mass," Handel's "Messiah" or Mendelssohn's "Elijah." More often, two or three works are offered. A typical varied program: the Fauré "Requiem," Vaughan Williams' "Mass in G," and Vivaldi's "Gloria."

Programs are usually conducted with more emphasis on fun than finesse.

See newspapers and listen to radio stations with community bulletin boards for announcements.

48

Chapter 4

SINGING HINTS

"Song ascends the heavens faster than prayer."

Chassidic adage

SINGING HINTS

This book won't attempt to teach you the mechanics of singing. For that we recommend a voice teacher who will be there in person to correct any bad habits you may pick up. No book can do that.

What we can and will offer in the next few pages are helpful, non-controversial hints on diction, breathing and posture as they apply to choral singers.

Diction

Diction, as defined by the American Academy of Teachers of Singing, is a combination of pronunciation, enunciation and articulation.

"*Pronunciation* is the utterance of words with regard to sound and accent. *Enunciation* is the manner of utterance as regards fullness and clearness. *Articulation* is the action of the speech organs in the formation of consonants, vowels, syllables and words. Correct pronunciation, enunciation and articulation in singing constitute Good Diction."

In group singing, diction must be uniform. Where your version of a sound differs from the conductor's, use his, even if it hurts. Remember that a chorus is not a democracy as far as pronunciation and interpretation are concerned. If it is not a question of judgment, however, and you are sure the conductor is wrong, you can tactfully bring it to his attention.

Vowels, consonants, final consonants and diphthongs should be uniform throughout the chorus regarding duration and sound. Attacks and releases must be synchronized. This can only be accomplished if *everyone* watches the conductor.

If the text of the work is in a foreign language, your conductor will undoubtedly review the pronunciation of the words before you sing them. Mark your music immediately so you won't forget from one week to the next. If you are proficient in a language the conductor does not know, he will welcome your help.

In the case of Latin texts, there is no universally accepted set of pronunciation rules today. If you are accustomed to pronouncing the word DEO "day-oh," and your conductor wants "deh-oh," do it his way.

Enunciate clearly. Listeners want to hear and understand what you are singing.

"Mood" or "interpretation" should be added to the definition of enunciation. "Fullness and clearness" are of little value if the performance is bland. Study the text and be aware at all times of the meaning of the words you are singing. Color your voice to convey the meaning of those words. Get your message across to the audience.

Vowels: Generally, only vowels are sustained in singing. The exceptions, at the discretion of the conductor, are the consonants "l," "m," "n" and "ng." This "Fred Waring" effect is often used in popular music. In classical music it is used subtly and sparingly. For example, your conductor may ask you to "sing through" these consonants so that they may be heard more clearly by the audience.

A vowel is held as long as possible before pronouncing the consonant it precedes:

Fig. 28

Compound Vowels: Hold the first part of the sound as *long* as possible.

> A as in May: eh' - ee
> I as in cry: ah' - ee
> O as in flow: oh' - oo

In the following sound, the first part of the sound is as *short* as possible:

> OO as in few, view, cue: ee - oo'.

Diphthongs: Hold the first part of the sound as long as possible:

> OI   oil
>   as in   : aw' - ee
> OY   boy
>
> OU   loud
>   as in   : ah' - oo
> OW   how

Fig. 29

Written

Sung

Consonants: There are two kinds of consonants, voiced and unvoiced.

The voiced consonant sounds are b, d, g (as in gem), j, l, m, n, r, v, w, z, ng, th (thou), y (ye) and the sound zh (plea̲sure).

These consonants take longer to articulate than the unvoiced consonants and must be started in time for the vowel following to be sung precisely when it should sound. The aspirate h, although unvoiced, falls within this category.

The unvoiced consonant sounds are f, k, p, s, t, th (thank), ch and sh. These are pronounced almost simultaneously with the vowel they precede.

Pitfalls in Pronouncing Consonants: If you don't articulate voiced consonants properly, they come out sounding like their unvoiced equivalents.

For example, "Deo" becomes "Teo," "very" becomes "ferry," etc.

Watch your "ng"s and "wh"s. Sing "bringing," not "bringin' "; sing "white" as "hwite," not "wite."

Think consonants on the same pitch as the vowels they precede. Don't scoop up to the note.

Consonants do not carry as well as vowels and must be pronounced more loudly than vowels in order to be heard equally well. Singing them in this manner may sound exaggerated to you, but not to the audience.

Breathing

An obvious fact we often overlook is that choral music was written for choruses rather than individual voices. The composer often makes demands in choral lines that individual voices cannot handle.

For example, some notes are held far beyond the breath capacity of the average singer. Phrases may run bar after bar with no natural place to take a breath. As one singer aptly put it: "There ain't no swallerin' room."

So—if you can't sing a phrase in one breath, don't feel infe-
rior or inadequate. Simply breathe where you have to, and if
possible, where it will do the least harm to the phrase.

In a long phrase, unless your conductor specifically asks
for no breath, try to breathe while your neighbor is singing.
He/she will breathe while you are singing. The effect to the audience, as the composer intended all along, will be one of
continuous sound.

When there are no rests, don't break the rhythm to
breathe, but "steal" time from a note, especially before an attack note.

If you run out of breath before finishing a word that ends
on a consonant, *don't pronounce the consonant.* Take a breath
and start singing again at the beginning of the next word. In this
way, you won't pronounce the consonant before other singers
who don't take a breath.

When you enter after "stealing" a breath, make sure
you're not singing more loudly than before the breath so that
the break is not noticeable.

Have the whole phrase in mind before the attack so that
you will have enough breath to complete it. Mark your copy at
the beginning of the phrase accordingly—"deep breath."

The text can dictate where breaths are to be taken. Punc-
tuation marks are usually good places. Although a slight break
is indicated at commas and semi-colons, your conductor has
the last word.

The last note of a phrase should be at the same dynamic
level as the first, unless otherwise indicated.

Posture

Good posture promotes mental alertness and should be
maintained at rehearsals and concerts.

Sitting

1. Feet. Both completely on the floor. *Never, never* cross
your legs or slouch with your legs stretched out in front of you.

2. Back. Straight, but not rigid. Sit forward toward the
edge of your seat. If this is too tiring, sit up straight against the
back of your seat.

3. Head. Level.

4. Hands. Hold up your music almost horizontally and
well in front of you with both hands, so that you can see the conductor and the music at the same time.

Standing

1. Feet. One slightly in front of the other or even with each other, pointing toward the conductor. Legs relaxed, slightly bent at the knees.
2. Back. Straight.
3. Head. Level.
4. Hands. As above.

Consciously relax your jaw, throat, lips, neck, tongue and chest.

Bring a Pencil to Every Rehearsal and Use It!

Chapter 5

ELEMENTS OF MUSIC
(Prelude to Sightsinging)

"By keeping my eyes and ears open, I soon
identify the few who are really able to read at
sight. . . . The rest is easy. I simply get beside one
of them, and sing what he sings. . . ."

George Bernard Shaw

You'd be surprised at the number of people who do as George Bernard Shaw did. If you *really* want to enjoy group singing, however, learn to be self-reliant.

There are people who can pick up a piece of music they've never seen before and read it as easily as a newspaper. This ability is called sightsinging. The rest of this book will be devoted to making you a sightsinger.

The material in the following pages is presented in slow and easy steps, with exercises along the way with which to test yourself. Make sure you understand each point before you go on to the next one. Take it in small doses, be patient, and remember your goal—you'll do fine.

Our musical forefathers had to contend with two main problems when they invented music notation:

1. How to indicate to the reader the length of time a sound is to be held (rhythm).
2. How to differentiate on paper between sounds (pitch).

RHYTHM

Rhythm is based on the beat.

What is a beat? It is the elapsed time from one tick of the clock up to, but not including, the next tick. For "one tick of the clock" you can substitute "one beat of your heart," "one click of your directional signal," etc.

Look at it another way. With your finger, start tapping in a slow but steady rhythm on this page. Sing "la" each time your finger touches the page. A beat is the elapsed time from one "la" up to, but not including, the next "la."

Let us assume in the following exercises that the quarter note (♩) represents one beat. Then a group of two beats would look like this, reading left to right:

Fig. 30

The vertical lines (| |) that enclose the group of beats above are called bar lines. The musical content between the bar lines is called a "bar" or "measure."

Say the following bar on the words "one, two" while tapping with your finger. The first beat ends when the second beat begins; the second beat ends at the bar line, where "one" of the next bar would begin.

Fig. 31   beginning of beat 1 → beginning of beat 2 → | (♩)
one   two   one

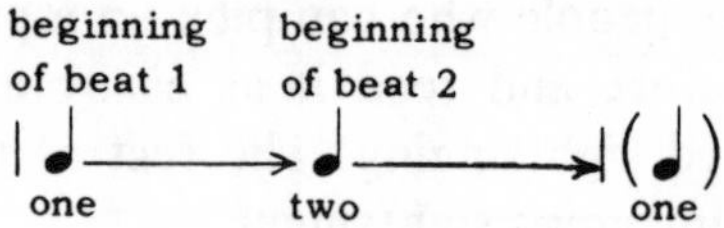

A bar may also contain three beats. Tap out and say on "one, two, three."

Fig. 32 | ♩——→♩——→♩——→| (♩)
one   two   three   one

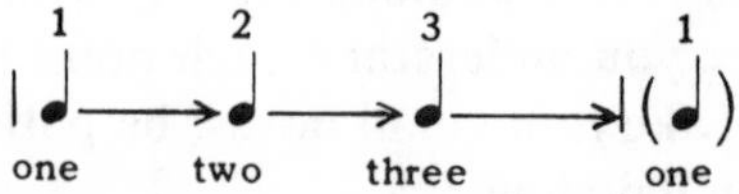

This is a bar of four beats. Tap out and say on "one, two, three, four."

Fig. 33 | ♩——→♩——→♩——→♩——→| (♩)
one   two   three   four   one

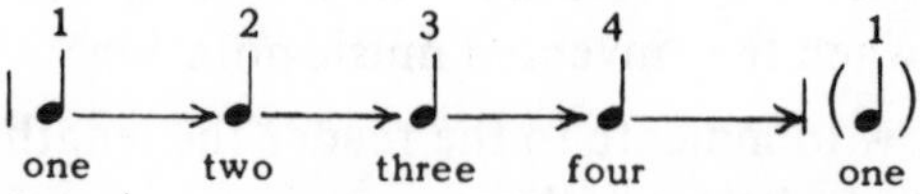

The half note (♩) is double the time value of the quarter note. If the quarter note lasts one beat, then the half note lasts two beats. In the following four-beat bar, tap out and say on "la," holding the first "la" the same length of time you said "one, two" above, and the second "la" the same length of time you said "three, four."

Fig. 34 | ♩————————→♩————————→| (♩)
la   la   la

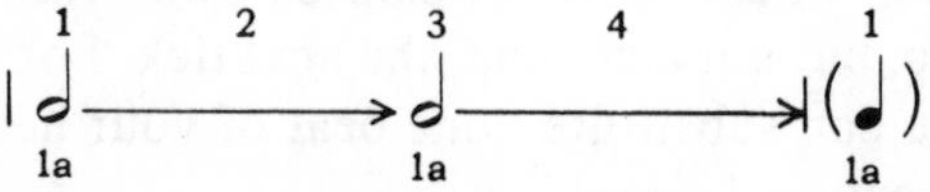

The whole note (o) lasts twice as long as the half note, in this case four beats. Tap out and say on "la," holding "la" the same length of time it took you to say "one, two, three, four" above.

Fig. 35 | o ————————————————→| (♩)
la   la

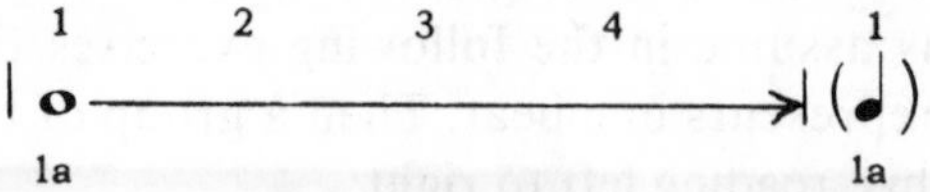

The single beat, in this case the quarter note, can be subdivided into two equal parts. It's simple arithmetic: a quarter note equals two eighth notes. The eighth note looks like a quarter note with one flag on its stem: (♪).

This is a four beat bar in eighth notes. (♪ ♪ can also be written ♫ .)

Fig. 36 | ♪ ♪ ♪ ♪ ♪ ♪ ♪ ♪ |
1   2   3   4

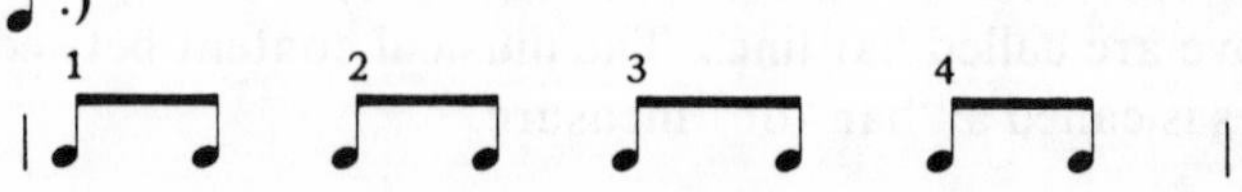

Tap out the following bar at the same speed (tempo) you've been using all along and say "one-and, two-and, three-and, four-and." "One" is said when your finger touches the page (↓), "and" is said when your finger is at its highest point off the page (↑); "two" is said when your finger touches the page again, etc.

From this point on, we will omit the horizontal arrow indicating that the last note in the bar should be held to the bar line, but don't forget to do it.

Fig. 37

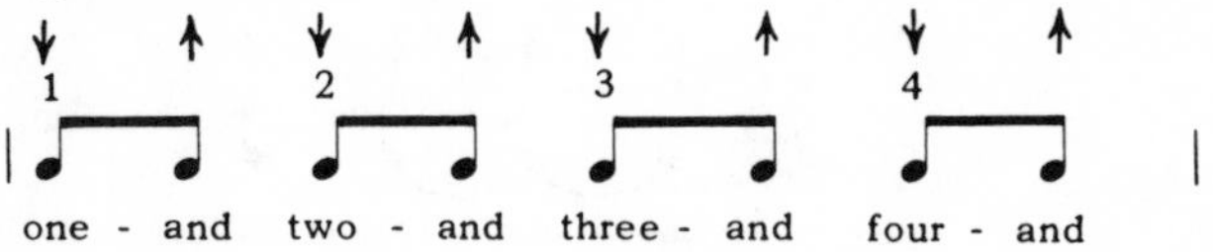

one - and   two - and   three - and   four - and

The vowel sound of the downbeat (↓) *begins* when your finger touches the page; the vowel sound of the upbeat (↑) *begins* when your finger is at its highest point off the page.

The beat, here the quarter note, may also be subdivided into four parts: four sixteenth notes. The sixteenth note looks like a quarter note with two flags on its stem: (♬). Two sixteenth notes may be written ♬ and four sixteenth notes may be written ♬♬ . Tap out the same tempo as in eighths, saying two syllables to each downbeat and two syllables to each upbeat.

Fig. 38

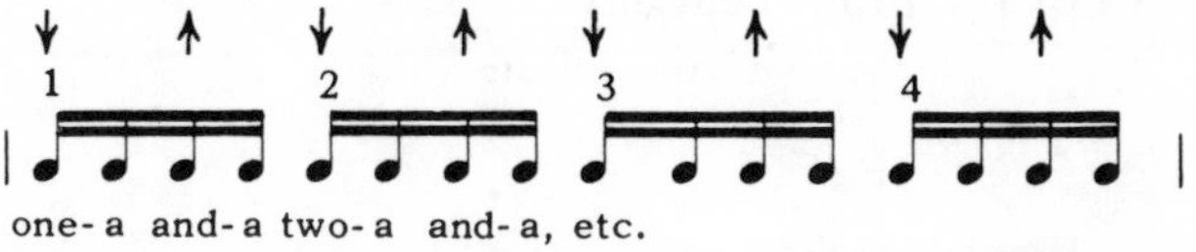

one- a and- a two- a and- a, etc.

There are also thirty-second notes with three flags on a stem (♪), and sixty-fourth notes with four flags on a stem (♪), but they will seldom occur in your music.

Dotted Notes

The dot adds one half the time value of the note preceding it to the note itself:

o. dotted whole note   = o + d
d. dotted half note   = d + d
d. dotted quarter note = d + ♪
♪. dotted eighth note = ♪ + ♪

Dotted notes seem trickier to read, but become simple when broken down. What is the rhythm of this two beat bar?

Fig. 39

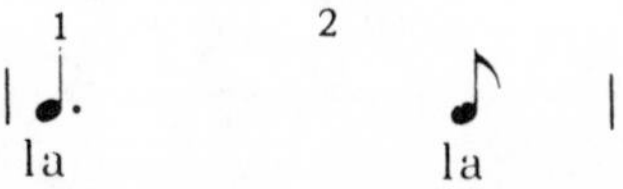

la   la

First, let's break down the bar to the note of shortest duration within it, the eighth note in this case:

Fig. 39a

The ties, (‿) or (⁀), indicate that the notes they connect are to be sounded as one note with the total value of all.

Next, divide each beat into downbeat and upbeat:

Fig. 39b

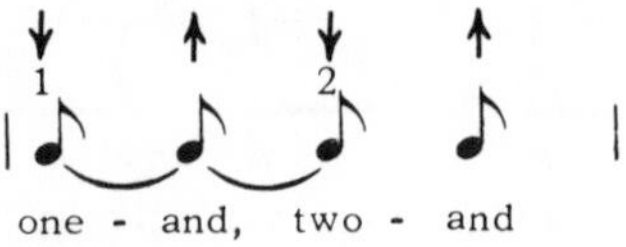

one - and, two - and

Compare with the original:

Fig. 39c

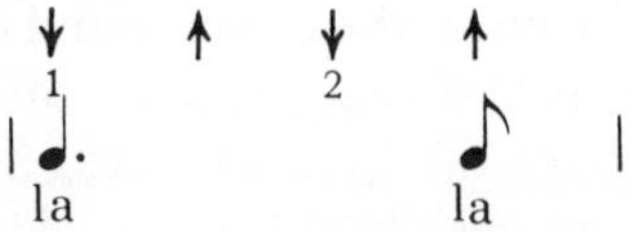

la   la

We can now see that ♩. gets all of the first beat and half of the second ("one-and, two-") or one and a half beats, and ♪ gets the second half of the second beat ("and"), or one-half beat.

Let's try a four beat bar:

one beat   three beats

Fig. 40

Breakdown:

Fig. 40a

one   two   three   four

Therefore, ♩ · is held for the time it would take to say "two, three, four," or three beats.

Exercises: beat out these bars by tapping your fingers against a hard surface and say on "la":

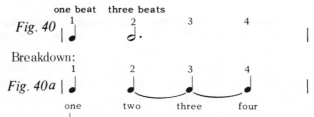

4 beat bar:

Fig. 41

la   la   la   la

3 beat bar:

Fig. 42

la   la

Rests

Music is a combination of sound and silence. Each note symbol has a corresponding symbol for silence (rest), which has the same duration as the note.

Sound	*Note*	*Silence* (rest)
♩	quarter note	𝄽
𝅗𝅥	half note	▬
o	whole note	▬
♪	eighth note	𝄾
♬	sixteenth note	𝄿
𝅘𝅥𝅲	thirty-second note	𝅀

Time Signatures

We already know that a group of beats is enclosed within two vertical bar lines. In your music, you may come across bars which have anywhere from one to twelve beats. Instead of the quarter note, the eighth note or the half note may get one beat. Then how can we tell how many beats there are in a bar and the name of the note which gets one beat? All the information is contained in the "time signature."

The time signature consists of two numbers. The top number tells you the number of beats in the bar, and the bottom number gives you the name of the note which gets one beat. For example:

$\begin{array}{c}4\\4\end{array}$	4 beats to the bar quarter note gets one beat
$\begin{array}{c}3\\8\end{array}$	3 beats to the bar eighth note gets one beat
$\begin{array}{c}3\\2\end{array}$	3 beats to the bar half note gets one beat

The $\frac{4}{4}$ bar contains a total of four quarter notes in any combination, such as two half notes, one whole note, etc.; the $\frac{3}{8}$ bar contains a total of three eighth notes in any combination, and the $\frac{3}{2}$ bar contains a total of three half notes in any combination.

For example:

Fig. 43 | 4/4 ♩ ♩ ♩ 𝄽 ‖ 𝅗𝅥 𝅗𝅥 ‖ 𝅗𝅥. ♩ |

| 3/8 ♪ ♪ ♪ ‖ 𝅗𝅥 ♪ ‖ 𝅗𝅥. |

| 3/2 𝅗𝅥 𝅝 ‖ 𝅝. ‖ 𝅗𝅥 𝅗𝅥 ▬ |

Accents

Implicit in the time signature is the way the beats within the bar are to be accented (stressed).

Composers use these symbols when they want to give a note a special emphasis: ∧ or >, as in

But even if there are no written accent marks in a bar, there are certain accent values inherent in each beat. For example, the first beat in each bar will normally get the heaviest accent in the bar.

To demonstrate accents, we will use the following signs.

     ❜ heavy

     ╱ light

     ◡ unaccented

In a 2/4 bar or a 2/2 bar, the first beat is accented, the second unaccented:

Fig. 44 | 2/4 ♩ ♩ |

               | 2/2 𝅗𝅥 𝅗𝅥 |

In a 4/4 bar, the first beat gets the heaviest accent, the third is lightly accented, and the second and fourth are unaccented:

Fig. 45 | 4/4 ♩ ♩ ♩ ♩ |

In a 3/2, 3/4, and 3/8 bar, the first beat is heavily accented and the second and third beats are unaccented:

Fig. 46 | 3/2 𝅗𝅥 𝅗𝅥 𝅗𝅥 ‖ 3/4 ♩ ♩ ♩ ‖ 3/8 ♪ ♪ ♪ |

A $\frac{6}{8}$ bar is accented as follows:

Fig. 47 | $\frac{6}{8}$

A $\frac{9}{8}$ bar:

Fig. 48 | $\frac{9}{8}$

A $\frac{12}{8}$ bar:

Fig. 49 | $\frac{12}{8}$

Syncopation

When a note occurring on an unaccented beat is added to a note occurring on an accented beat, that note is accented (syncopation). For example:

Fig. 50 Unsyncopated

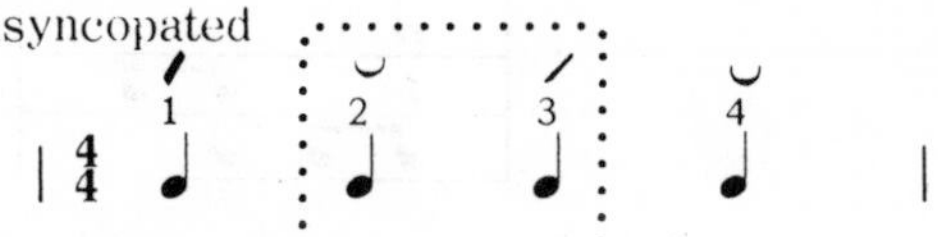

Fig. 50a Syncopated

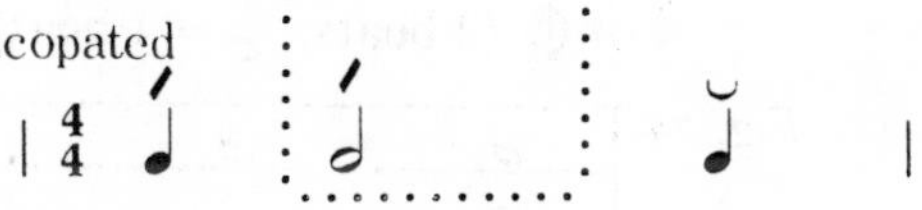

The 𝅗𝅥 occurs on beat 2, normally unaccented.

Or:

Fig. 51 Unsyncopated:

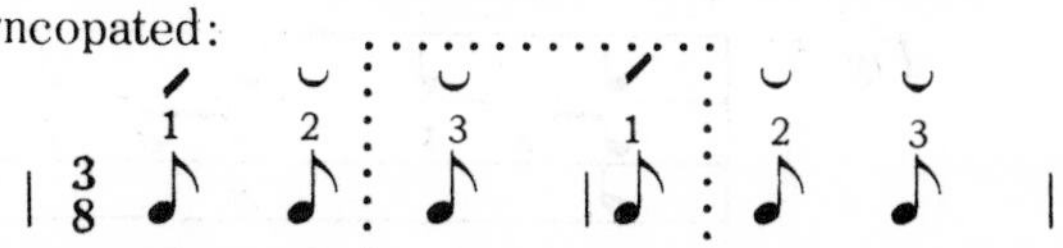

Fig. 51a Syncopated:

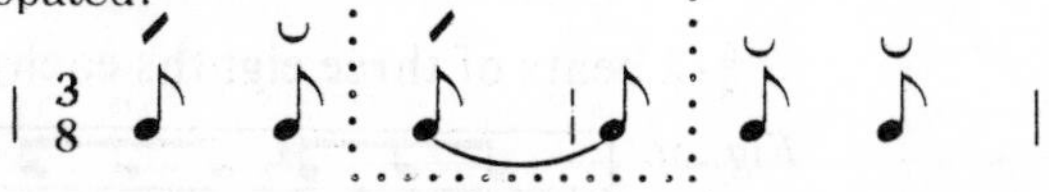

The tied eighth note (♪♪) occurs on beat three, normally an unaccented beat.

Exercise: **Tap out these bars and say on "la," observing the accents:**

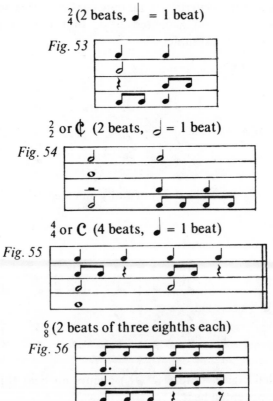

Groups of beats may come in multiples of two or three or combinations of both.

Two and Its Multiples

Study, then tap out and say each of the following bars on "la."

$\frac{12}{8}$ (4 beats of three eighths each)

Fig. 57

Three and Its Multiples

Study, then tap out and say each of the following bars on "la":

$\frac{3}{4}$ (3 beats, ♩ = 1 beat)

Fig. 58

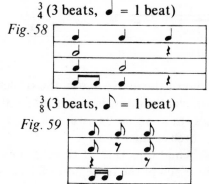

$\frac{3}{8}$ (3 beats, ♪ = 1 beat)

Fig. 59

$\frac{9}{8}$ (3 beats of three eighths each) $\frac{3}{2}$ (3 beats, ♩ = 1 beat)

Fig. 60   *Fig. 61*

Combinations

$\frac{5}{4}$ is $\frac{3}{4} + \frac{2}{4}$ or $\frac{2}{4} + \frac{3}{4}$. The composer indicates the separation by a vertical dotted line.

$\frac{5}{4}$ (♩ = 1 beat)

Fig. 62

$\frac{7}{4}$ is $\frac{4}{4} + \frac{3}{4}$ or $\frac{3}{4} + \frac{4}{4}$.

$\frac{7}{4}$ (♩ = 1 beat)

Fig. 63

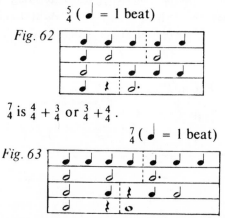

Triplets

Another rhythm pattern is the triplet, where a group of three notes is sung in the same length of time it would take to sing two notes of the same duration.

The triplet is usually indicated by a "3" in the case of eighth notes, a brace and "3" in the case of quarter notes.

Fig. 64

In the first bar of the above figure, the triplet is sung in the time value of two eighth notes; in the second bar, the triplet is sung in the same time value as two quarter notes. You are actually beating three against two.

Here is a schematic picture of three against two, moving from left to right. Each of the three notes falls in a precise place in time:

Fig. 64 a

Using both hands, beat three against two. Let your left hand represent the "three" and your right hand the "two." Saying the phrase "three into two" will help you get the rhythm:

Fig. 64 b

left hand:

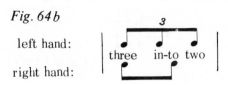

three   in-to two

right hand:

PITCH

If you had to describe the sound of a note on paper, how would you go about it? Think for a moment . . . difficult, isn't it? Fortunately, the same musical forefathers who worked it out so beautifully for rhythm also did it for pitch. Here is the system as it is today:

There are two sets of horizontal lines, five lines to each set, with a fragment of a line between them. Each set of five lines is called a staff, the two staves together comprise the Great (Grand) Staff.

Each line and space has a name. The names of musical notes are these letters: A, B, C, D, E, F and G. They are written consecutively, upwards from the bottom of the staff, with one letter for each line and space.

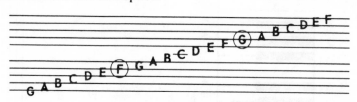

Since the two staves are not alike (the lines and spaces have different names), how can we tell one from the other? We add a symbol called the clef sign.

The G clef symbol (𝄞) is written with one end touching the second line from the bottom of the staff (G). You will recognize this as the upper half of the Great Staff. It is also known as the treble clef.

Fig. 65

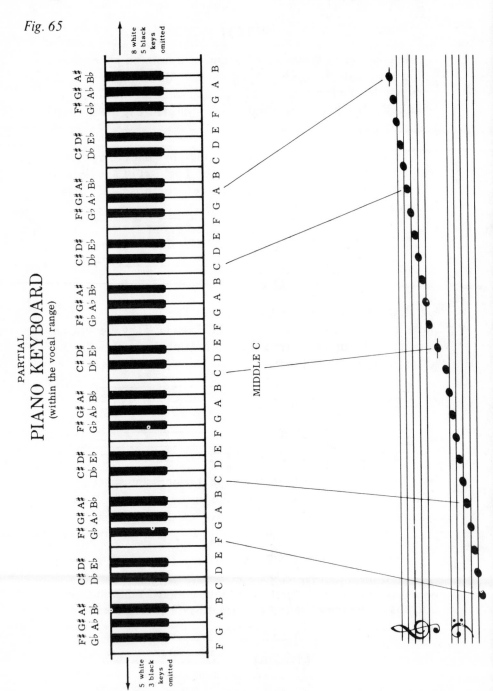

PARTIAL
PIANO KEYBOARD
(within the vocal range)

MIDDLE C

Knowing that the second line (always counting from the bottom up) is G tells us the names of all the lines and spaces in relation to G.

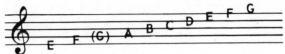

The lines of the treble clef are EGBDF and can be remembered by the sentence "Every Good Boy Does Fine." The spaces spell the word "FACE."

Notes below and above the staff may be added by drawing fragments of lines. These are called "leger" lines. With leger lines below and above, the G clef looks like this:

The F clef (𝄢) is written with one end touching the fourth line from the bottom (F) of the lower half of the Great Staff, and two dots straddling the F line. This is also called the bass clef.

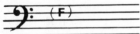

With extensions below and above, the F clef looks like this:

The lines of the bass clef are GBDFA, "Gentlemen Basses Don't Follow Altos." The spaces are ACEG: "All Cows Eat Grass" or "All Cars Eat Gas."

If you look at the piano keyboard on the opposite page, you see that the white keys are named A, B, C, D, E, F and G. What are the names of the black keys?

C D E F G A B C

Music of the western world is made up of twelve different tones, equally spaced from each other. The smallest unit of distance between any two tones (notes) is called the half-step. In the figure above, from C to the black key above and to the right of it is a half-step. From the same black key to D is also a half-step, and so on.

What happens between E and F and B and C, which are not separated by a black key? *They are already half-steps*. This is very important to remember when you come to the Interval Method of reading music later in this book.

Exercise: On your instrument, play the notes from C to C, including all the black and white keys. Hear how evenly the notes rise in pitch. Play them backwards and hear how evenly the notes fall in pitch.

How did those ancient musical geniuses cope with the problem of indicating in writing the half-steps between C–D, D–E, F–G, G–A, A–B, since there are no letters between the pairs? They invented two symbols called the sharp and the flat.

The sharp, which looks like a slightly askew tic-tac-toe game, raises a note one-half step:

For example, C sharp, the note between C and D, looks like this on the staff:

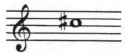

The sharp is written before the note.

The flat, which lowers a note one-half step in pitch, resembles a lower-case b:

The note one-half step lower than D is D♭.

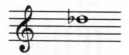

The flat is written before the note.

Looking at the piano keyboard, you may be surprised to see that C♯ and D♭ are the same key. Then why, you rightly ask, does it have two names? There is a logical but rather complicated reason called "enharmonic spelling," which we won't have to worry about. (Be aware that in using the letter name of a note, ♯ or ♭ is written after the letter: C♯, D♭.)

The figure on Page 66 shows you the location of the notes of the Great Staff on the piano.

Exercise: locate these notes on the piano.

Learn the names of the lines and spaces of the treble and bass clefs. If your time is limited, begin by learning only the clef on which your music appears:

- The treble clef for soprano and alto.
- The bass clef for basses and baritones.

Tenor music is most frequently written on the treble clef, but may also be written on the bass clef. Sorry, men.

Both clefs should be learned by all choral singers so that they can find their cues from the other voice parts or the accompaniment.

SCALES

Do you remember the "do, re, mi, fa, sol, la, ti, do" exercises you sang in elementary school? That was a "scale" you were singing. A major scale, to be exact. Learning how scales are built will help you learn to sightsing.

A major scale is a group of eight consecutive notes, the first seven having different names and the eighth having the same name as the first, in a prescribed arrangement of whole and half-steps. Let's tear that statement apart and say it in English.

". . . eight consecutive notes, the first seven having different names and the eighth having the same name as the first." For example, from C to C.

1	2	3	4	5	6	7	8
C	D	E	F	G	A	B	C

A "whole step"? We already know that a half-step is the distance between any note and the note on the piano closest to it in pitch. A whole step consists of two consecutive half-steps. For example, from C to C♯ is a half-step; from C♯ to D is a half-step; therefore, from C to D is a whole step.

The Major Scale

There are eight notes in the major scale. From now on we'll call them "degrees": the first note is the 1st degree, the second note is the 2nd degree, etc.

All major scales are built on the same pattern.

It's like a garment pattern. You can make two dresses using different materials from the same pattern. Although the materials may be different, both dresses will have exactly the same shape.

Woodworkers know that pieces cut to the same template will be identical in shape whether they're made of pine, oak or maple.

In all major scales, the distances between the degrees follow the same pattern, no matter which note you start with.

The distance from the 1st degree to the 2nd degree is always one whole step; from the 2nd to the 3rd degree is always one whole step; from the 3rd to the 4th degree is always a half step; from the 4th to the 5th degree is always one whole step; from the 5th to the 6th degree is always one whole step; from the 6th to the 7th is always one whole step; from the 7th to the 8th degree is always one half step.

Putting it all together, the pattern of the major scale is

$$1 \quad 1 \quad \tfrac{1}{2} \quad 1 \quad 1 \quad 1 \quad \tfrac{1}{2}$$
$$1 \quad 2 \quad 3 \;\; 4 \quad 5 \quad 6 \quad 7 \;\; 8$$

Using this pattern, let's build the key of C major (the major scale that starts on C).

First, write the pattern on a separate piece of paper. Note that the spaces between 3–4 and 7–8, where the half-steps occur, are half the length of the others. ⌣ indicates the half-step.

Next, write the name of the first degree of the scale (C) under 1:

$$1 \quad 1 \quad \tfrac{1}{2} \quad 1 \quad 1 \quad 1 \quad \tfrac{1}{2}$$
$$1 \quad 2 \quad 3 \;\; 4 \quad 5 \quad 6 \quad 7 \;\; 8$$
$$C$$

According to the pattern, there should be one whole step from 1 to 2. Count a whole step from C, using your instrument if you wish. C to C♯ is a half-step, C♯ to D is a half-step, therefore D is a whole step from C. Write D under 2.

From 2 to 3 there should be a whole step. Count one whole step from D. D to D♯ is a half-step, D♯ to E is a half-step, therefore D to E is a whole step. Write E under 3.

From 3 to 4 there should be a half-step. From E to F *is* a half-step. Write F under 4.

Complete the rest of the scale on your own. The answer is below, but don't cheat!*

The key of C was easy. Let's try another. Using the pattern, build the major scale beginning on G.

The first six degrees contain no surprises, but then something new happens. Between 6 and 7 there should be a whole step, but E to F is only a half-step. Therefore a half-step has to be added to F to fit the pattern. This is accomplished by raising F one half-step to F♯. Write F♯ under 7. From 7 to 8 there should be a half-step, and F♯ to G nicely fills the bill.

Let's try one more example of a major scale: the key of F major.

```
      1       1      ½     1       1       1      ½
    /   \   /   \   /  \  /   \   /   \   /   \  /  \
  1       2       3    4       5       6       7    8
  F       G       A    ?
```

What happens between 3 and 4? For 4 we need a half-step from A, but B is a whole step from A. Therefore a half-step must be subtracted from B by flatting it (B♭). The complete scale of the key of F major is:

```
      1       1      ½     1       1       1      ½
    /   \   /   \   /  \  /   \   /   \   /   \  /  \
  1       2       3    4       5       6       7    8
  F       G       A   B♭      C       D       E    F
```

Why didn't we call 4 "A♯," which is also a half step from A? Remember the definition of the major scale: ". . . eight consecutive notes, the first seven having *different* names . . ." If we had used A♯ for 4, then we would have had two notes of the *same* name (A, A♯).

Play the keys of C, G and F major on your instrument. Learn to recognize the distinctive "melody" of the major scale.

By following the pattern, you can now build any major scale.

Key: A key is a scale named after the first note of that scale. For example, the major scale which starts on G is the key of G major.

Exercise 1: build the following major keys. Remember that half-steps occur between 3–4 and 7–8; all the others are whole steps.

```
  1     2     3  4     5     6     7  8

  A
  E
  B
  B♭
  E♭
  A♭
```

(Answers will be found at the end of this section).

Key Signatures

The key signature of a piece of music tells us where the sharps or flats occur in the key. The ♯ on the F line below means that every note on the F line or space should be sung F♯. This is the key of G major: one sharp.

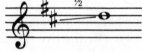

There is also a minor key with one sharp (E minor), which we will discuss later.

You can memorize the key signatures on Page 114, or learn this mechanical way of determining a key from a key signature.

Sharp keys: the key note is a half-step up from the sharp furthest to the right.

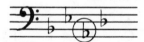

Flat keys: the second flat from the right is the key note.

Since the key of C has no sharps or flats, and the key of F has only one flat, they will have to be memorized.

Minor Scales

For every major key there is a corresponding (relative) minor key. Their key signatures are exactly the same. The only difference is that the minor scale begins on the sixth degree of the major scale.

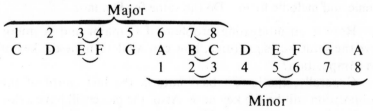

Exercise 2: find the relative minor keys of

     D major
     F major
     G major
     B♭ major

The pattern of a relative minor key is:

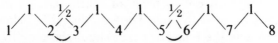

This is called the "natural" minor scale. The key of A minor in its natural form is:

1	2⌣3	4	5⌣6	7	8
A	B⌣C	D	E⌣F	G	A

Play the above scale on your instrument. It has a rather bland sound and is often altered to give it more spice.

In the "harmonic" form of the minor scale, the 7th degree is raised a half step:

1	2⌣3	4	5⌣6	7⌣8
A	B⌣C	D	E⌣F	G♯ A

Play the A minor harmonic scale on your instrument. The raised 7th degree gives it a distinctive new flavor.

The "melodic" form of the minor scale raises both the 6th and 7th degrees one half step:

1	2⌣3	4	5	6	7⌣8
A	B⌣C	D	E	F♯	G♯ A

This form ascending begins like a minor scale and ends like a major scale. The "melodic" minor scale descending is like the natural minor scale:

Exercise 3: spell out the key of E minor in its natural, harmonic and melodic forms. Do the same for D minor.

Here is an interesting problem: if C major and A minor have the same key signatures, how can we determine the key of the composition?

Generally, the lowest bass note in the last chord of the composition will be the key note. Also, the piece will have a distinctly major or minor sound in most cases.

Here is a mechanical way of finding a relative minor key: count one and a half steps back from the 8th degree of its major scale.

Or, the name of the 6th degree of a major scale is the name of its relative minor key.

ANSWERS TO EXERCISES

Exercise 1:

1	2	3⌣4		5	6	7⌣8	
A	B	C♯	D	E	F♯	G♯	A
E	F♯	G♯	A	B	C♯	D♯	E
B	C♯	D♯	E	F♯	G♯	A♯	B
B♭	C	D	E♭	F	G	A	B♭
E♭	F	G	A♭	B♭	C	D	E♭
A♭	B♭	C	D♭	E♭	F	G	A♭

Exercise 2:
D major - B minor
F major - D minor
G major - E minor
B♭ major - G minor

Exercise 3:

E minor:
    Natural: E, F♯, G, A, B, C, D, E.
    Harmonic: E, F♯, G, A, B, C, D♯, E.
    Melodic (ascending): E, F♯, G, A, B, C♯, D♯, E.
          (descending): E, D♮, C♮, B, A, G, F♯, E.

D minor:
    Natural: D, E, F, G, A, B♭, C, D.
    Harmonic: D, E, F, G, A, B♭, C♯, D.
    Melodic (ascending): D, E, F, G, A, B♮, C♯, D.
          (descending): D, C♮, B♭, A, G, F, E, D.

Note the B♭ and C♯ in the key of D minor harmonic. Only the B♭ will appear in the key signature. A "♯" will be written in front of each C as it occurs in the composition.

Chapter 6

SIGHTSINGING

"Music is the universal language of mankind."

Longfellow

You now have the music theory you need for sightsinging. All that remains is ear training.

There are two important ear training tools. We'll call them the "1,2,3" Method and the Interval Method. You should know both, since each works better than the other in certain situations.

For example, you would use the "1,2,3" Method mainly in reading music in a major key and containing no sharps or flats other than those in the key signature. The Interval Method, which may be used for all melodies, is most useful in reading a melody in a minor key, one that changes keys, or one with many added sharps and flats.

"1,2,3" Method

We've all had the experience of singing with groups of people at parties or religious services and thinking that the songs or hymns were either "too high" or "too low" for our voices.

If the range is too high, we know that starting the song on a lower note will also lower the high notes. If the range is too low, we know that starting on a higher note will raise the low notes for us.

The underlying assumption we are making here is that it doesn't matter in which key we sing the song, the melody will always remain the same.

For example, let's try "Three Blind Mice" in two different keys.

Play and sing the first two bars of "Three Blind Mice" in the key of C:

Fig. 66

Three blind mice,   three blind mice

Now play and sing it in the key of G:

Fig. 66a

Three blind mice,   three blind mice

Although the keys are different, the melody is the same.

The same is true of major scales. You can start a major scale on any one of twelve different notes and the "melody" will always be the same.

Play and sing the key of D (the major scale beginning on **D**) on the numbers "1,2,3,4,5,6,7,8."

Fig. 67

1   2   3   4   5   6   7   8

Now play and sing the key of C major:

Fig. 67a

1   2   3   4   5   6   7   8

Although the keys of D and C start on different notes, the "melody" is the same. Once you know the "melody" of one major scale, you know them all.

Play, Sing Exercises

These exercises will help you learn the sound of all degrees in relation to the 1st degree (1).

In the key of C, for example, every note on the C line or space will be 1, every note on the D line or space will be 2, and so on.

1   2   3   4   5   6   7   8(1)

Note that the degree numbers get higher from the bottom up. Each line and space represents one degree.

Let's do what we'll call the "Play, Sing Exercises" in C major together as an example.

First, play 1–8 in the key of C. Sing the numbers as you play. Concentrate on the "melody." Correlate the name and number of each note with its place on the staff.

Exercise 1

1   2   1

Play 1 (C). Sing 1. Sing 2 (D). Play 2 to see if you've sung it correctly. Then sing 1. Play 1.

Go on to the next exercise when you know this one well.

Exercise 2

1   (2)   3   (2)   1

Play 1. Sing 1. Think 2. Sing 3. Play 3. Think 2. Sing 1. Play 1.

The object of this exercise is to sing 1 and then 3 without singing 2. In the beginning it will be easier if you "think" 2 in passing on the way to 3. Sing aloud "one," sing mentally "two," sing aloud "three."

First do this exercise "thinking" 2, then without thinking 2. Five times each will do as a starter. Remember, however, that the more time you spend on these very important ear-training sessions, the faster you will become a good sightsinger.

Sightsing the following melodies. If at first it is too difficult for you to do both the melody and the rhythm, do the melody only. Figure all degrees from 1, which is given in each example. Play 1 on your instrument. Sing on the number of the scale. (Do all sightsinging exercises in your own range.)

SIGHTSINGING EXERCISES

Exercise 3

Play 1. Sing 1. Think 2,3. Sing 4. Play 4. Think 3,2. Sing 1. Play 1.

Sing this exercise five times thinking 2,3; sing five times without thinking 2,3.

Sightsing these melodies. Play 1 on your instrument. If you haven't been able to sightsing the melodies following Play, Sing Exercises 1 and 2, give them more time before attempting those below.

SIGHTSINGING EXERCISES

Exercise 4

Play 1. Sing 1. Think 2,3,4. Sing 5. Play 5. Think 4,3,2. Sing 1. Play 1.

Sing this exercise five times thinking 2,3,4; sing five times without thinking 2,3,4.

Sightsing these melodies. Play 1 on your instrument. Have you mastered the melodies with degrees 1 through 4?

SIGHTSINGING EXERCISES

Exercise 5

Play 1. Sing 1. Think 2,3,4,5. Sing 6. Play 6. Think 5,4,3,2. Sing 1. Play 1. Sing five times thinking 2,3,4,5; sing five times without thinking 2,3,4,5.

Sightsing the following melodies. Play 1 on your instrument. If you have not as yet mastered degrees 1 through 5, go back to them before trying this exercise.

SIGHTSINGING EXERCISES

Exercise 6

1 (2 3 4 5 6) 7 (6 5 4 3 2) 1

Play 1. Sing 1. Think 2,3,4,5,6. Sing 7. Play 7. Think 6,5,4,-3,2. Sing 1. Play 1.

Sing this exercise five times thinking 2,3,4,5,6; sing five times without thinking 2,3,4,5,6.

Exercise 7

1 (2 3 4 5 6 7) 8 (7 6 5 4 3 2) 1

Play 1. Sing 1. Think 2,3,4,5,6,7. Sing 8. Play 8. Think 7,6,-5,4,3,2. Sing 1. Play 1.

Sing this exercise five times thinking 2,3,4,5,6,7; sing five times without thinking 2,3,4,5,6,7.

If you have mastered degrees 1 through 6, sightsing these melodies. Play 1 on your instrument.

SIGHTSINGING EXERCISES

For additional practice, read the preceding sightsinging exercises in reverse (from the last note to the first).

PLAY, SING EXERCISES TABLE

Play 1–8 in a major key that is vocally comfortable for you. See keys below. Use different keys for variety. Sing the numbers.

Do each exercise five times thinking numbers in between, then five times without thinking numbers in between.

Ex. 1.	Play 1.	Sing 1.		Sing 2.	Play 2.	Sing 1.		Play 1.
Ex. 2.	Play 1. Sing 1.	(Think 2).	Sing 3.	Play 3.	(Think 2).	Sing 1.	Play 1.
Ex. 3.	Play 1. Sing 1.	(Think 2, 3).	Sing 4.	Play 4.	(Think 3, 2).	Sing 1.	Play 1.
Ex. 4.	Play 1. Sing 1.	(Think 2, 3,4).	Sing 5.	Play 5.	(Think 4, 3,2).	Sing 1.	Play 1.
Ex. 5.	Play 1. Sing 1.	(Think 2, 3,4,5).	Sing 6.	Play 6.	(Think 5, 4,3,2).	Sing 1.	Play 1.
Ex. 6.	Play 1. Sing 1.	(Think 2, 3,4,5,6).	Sing 7.	Play 7.	(Think 6, 5,4,3,2).	Sing 1.	Play 1.
Ex. 7.	Play 1. Sing 1.	(Think 2, 3,4,5,6,7).	Sing 8.	Play 8.	(Think 7, 6,5,4,3,2).	Sing 1.	Play 1.

Major Keys Comfortable for Most Voices

KEY	*1*	*2*	*3*	*4*	*5*	*6*	*7*	*8*
B♭ major	B♭	C	D	E♭	F	G	A	B♭
C major	C	D	E	F	G	A	B	C
D major	D	E	F♯	G	A	B	C♯	D
E♭ major	E♭	F	G	A♭	B♭	C	D	E♭

Use "Piano Keyboard" illustration on Page 66 to play scale, if necessary.

Do these exercises in the keys of the pieces you are rehearsing.

The Seven Steps

Suppose you are a beginner at sightsinging and want to read a piece of music* you are seeing for the first time. How would you go about it?

Here is the procedure in seven steps.

Let's take this melody as an example:

Fig. 68

Here's a lit-tle folk song, child-ren sing in France.

Step 1. Determine the key. If you don't as yet know the names of key signatures, see Page 114. Which key has one flat? F major or D minor. The lowest note of the last chord of the piece will almost always be the key note. In this case, the accompaniment would have told you that the key is F major.

Step 2. Spell out the key under the degree numbers of the scale.

1	2	3 4	5	6	7 8
F	G	A B♭	C	D	E F

Step 3. Tap out the rhythm and say on "la."

Step 4. Using the pattern in Step 2, locate all the degrees of the scale on the staff. Number the lines and spaces if necessary.

Fig. 68a

Here's a lit-tle folk song, child-ren sing in France.

Step 5. Play 1 on your instrument. (*No fair to play the rest of the melody!*)

Step 6. Remembering the sound of the other degrees in relation to 1, sing the melody on "la."

Step 7. Sing the melody with the words, paying attention to tempo and dynamic markings.

*In a major key and with no sharps or flats other than those in the key signature.

Let's try another melody, but this time we'll pretend that there is no musical instrument available to you.

Fig. 69

This is a joy-ful mel-o-dy, we sing at Christ-mas time.

Step 1. Determine the key. (The lowest note of the last chord is D.)

Step 2. Spell out the key under the degree numbers of the scale.

1	2	3	4	5	6	7	8
D	E	F♯	G	A	B	C♯	D

Step 3. Tap out the rhythm.

Step 4. Using the scale pattern in Step 2, locate all the degrees of the scale on the staff. Number the lines and spaces if necessary.

Fig. 69 a

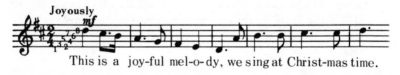

This is a joy-ful mel-o-dy, we sing at Christ-mas time.

Step 5. Instead of playing 1 on your instrument, hum any comfortable note and call it 1 or 8.

Step 6. Remembering the sound of the other degrees in relation to 1, sing the melody on "la."

Step 7. Sing the melody with the words, paying attention to tempo and dynamic markings.

Now play the melody and see how close you came to getting it right. Score 100% if the melody was correct, even if the key was not D.

When you become a proficient sightsinger, you will find yourself consciously doing only Steps 1 and 7. All the others will have become second nature to you.

In minor key melodies, or melodies with many sharps and/ or flats other than those in the key signature, Steps 1 through 5 are the same as above.

Step 6. If a minor melody has no sharps and/or flats added to degrees 1 through 5, the "1,2,3" Method will be effective for those degrees. The 6th and 7th degrees may be found by the Interval Method. Sing on "la."

For melodies with many added sharps and/or flats, the Interval Method is used for most notes. Sing on "la."

Step 7. Sing the melody with the words, paying attention to tempo and dynamic markings.

For additional practice, try reading simple music you may have around the house.

There are books of sightsinging exercises in any good music store. One of the best is *Melodia* (complete) by Cole and Lewis, published by Oliver Ditson Company.

We will discuss reading music in minor keys more fully in the section on the Interval Method of sightsinging.

Do these melodies on your own, using the Seven Steps:

(G minor)

Fig. 70

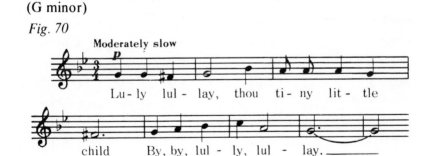

(C major)

Fig. 71

Interval Method

Glo - - - - - - - - - -

Obviously, the difficult skips and added sharps and naturals in the above example call for a tool other than the "1,2, 3" Method of sightsinging. That tool is the Interval Method.

In the "1,2,3" Method, every note relates to 1 of the piece. In the Interval Method, each note relates to the note immediately preceding it. In effect, each note in turn becomes the first note of an interval. In this method, the notes in a vocal part are like stepping stones in a stream: the first note serves as a jumping off place for the second note, the second note for the third note, and so on.

An interval is the distance in whole and half steps between two consecutive notes. *Every interval has a sound of its own.* From the smallest to the largest, these are the intervals you will most frequently encounter.

Interval Table

Interval	Distance	Abbreviation	Example
augmented prime	½ step	½	C to C♯
minor 2nd	½ step	½	C to D♭
major 2nd	1 whole step	1	C to D
minor 3rd	1½ steps	m 3	C to E♭
augmented 2nd		aug. 2 or +2	C to D♯
major 3rd	2 whole steps	3	C to E
perfect 4th	2½ steps	4	C to F
augmented 4th	3 whole steps	aug. 4 or +4	C to F♯
diminished 5th		♭5	C to G♭
perfect 5th	3½ steps	5	C to G
augmented 5th	4 whole steps	aug. 5 or +5	C to G♯
minor 6th		m 6	C to A♭
major 6th	4½ steps	6	C to A
minor 7th	5 whole steps	m 7	C to B♭
augmented 6th		aug. 6 or +6	C to A♯
major 7th	5½ steps	7	C to B
octave	6 whole steps	oct. or 8	C to C

Learning the sound of these intervals, ascending and descending, and recognizing them on the staff are the "secrets" of sightsinging. Play them over and over, until you know them blindfolded.

Seconds

Seconds are two consecutive notes and therefore have no lines or spaces between them on the staff. (Another way of determining the name of an interval is by counting the number of lines and spaces from one note to the other.)

There are three types of seconds (2nds), each with a different sound:

The major second, which has a distance of 1 whole step between the notes;

The minor second, which has a distance of a half step between the notes; and

The augmented second, which has a distance of one and a half steps between the notes.

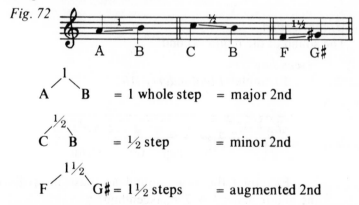

Fig. 72

In the following examples, the intervals are in parentheses.

The Major Second

The sound of the major second:

Ascending (going up from the bottom note):
Example: *Frère Jacques*

Frè - re   Jac - ques

Example: the same sound as the 1st to the 2nd degree (1–2) of the major scale ascending.

Descending (going down from the top note):
Example: *Three Blind Mice.*

Three   Blind   Mice

Example: the same sound as this interval in the major scale: 2–1, descending.

Practice and learn the sound of major 2nds, ascending and descending.

Exercise: play and sing each interval below five times, concentrating on the sound.

Fig. 73

The Minor Second

The sound of the minor second:

Ascending:
Example: *Londonderry Air*

My   gen - tle   harp

Example: the same sound as these intervals in the major scale: 3–4, 7–8, ascending.

Descending:
Example: *Joy to the World*

Joy   to   the   world

Example: the same sound as these intervals in the major scale: 4–3, 8–7, descending.

Practice and learn the sound of minor 2nds, ascending and descending.

Exercise: play and sing these intervals five times, concentrating on the sound.

Fig. 74

Are these two seconds the same?

Fig. 75

Play them and hear the difference. E–F, ½ step apart, comprise a minor 2nd; Eb–F, 1 whole step apart, comprise a major 2nd.

Cover the key signatures in the above examples and the intervals look exactly alike. Add the key signatures and they are different. That is why knowing keys and where whole and half-steps occur are important to sightsinging.

The Augmented Second

For the sound of the augmented second, see the Minor Third.

Determine whether the intervals below are major or minor seconds, mark as in the first interval, and sing on "la."

Fig. 76

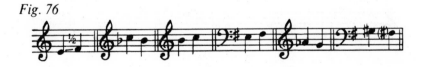

Thirds

Thirds have 1 line or 1 space between them on the staff.

There are two types of thirds:

The major 3rd, which has a distance of 2 whole steps between the notes; and

The minor 3rd, which has 1½ steps between the notes.

Fig. 77

The Major Third

The sound of the major 3rd:

Ascending:

Example: *The Blue Danube Waltz*

Oh   Da- nube so   blue

Example: the same sound as 1–3 in the major scale ascending.

Descending:

Example: *Swing Low, Sweet Chariot*

Swing Low,   Sweet Cha - ri - ot

Example: the same sound as 3–1 descending in the major scale.

Practice and learn the sound of major 3rds, ascending and descending.

Exercise: play and sing each interval five times and concentrate on the sound.

Fig. 78

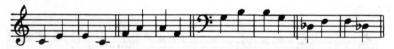

The Minor Third

The sound of the minor 3rd:

Ascending:

Example: *Greensleeves*

A - las my love you   do   me wrong

Example: the same sound as 6–8 ascending in the major scale.

Descending:

Example: *For He's a Jolly Good Fellow*

For he's a jol-ly good fel - low

Example: the same sound as 8-6 descending in the major scale.

Augmented 2nds sound exactly the same as minor 3rds. Breaking them down tells us why:

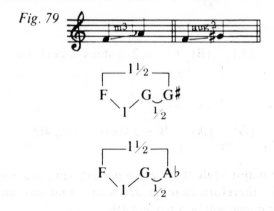

Fig. 79

Both are 1½ step intervals.

Practice and learn the sound of minor 3rds and augmented 2nds, ascending and descending.

If you find you can read minor 3rds more readily than augmented 2nds, don't hesitate to change your music:

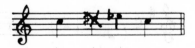

Determine whether the intervals below are major 3rds (2 whole steps), minor 3rds or augmented 2nds (1½ steps), mark, play and sing five times each.

Fig. 80

Fourths

Fourths have a total of 1 line and 1 space between them on the staff.

There are two types of 4ths:

The perfect 4th, with a distance of 2½ steps between the notes; and

The augmented 4th, with a distance of 3 whole steps between the notes.

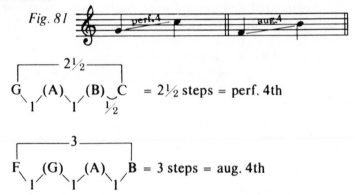

Fig. 81

In the major scale there are 6 perfect 4ths and only 1 augmented 4th, therefore chances are 6 to 1 that any fourth you find in your music will be a perfect 4th.

The Perfect Fourth

The sound of the perfect fourth:

Ascending:

Example: *Auld Lang Syne*

Should auld   ac - quaint-ance

Example: the same sound as 1–4 ascending in the major scale.

Descending:

Example: *Hallelujah Chorus* from Handel's "Messiah."

Hal - le - lu - jah

Example: the same sound as 4–1 descending in the major scale.

Practice and learn the sound of perfect 4ths, ascending and descending.

Exercise: play and sing these intervals five times each, concentrating on the sound.

Fig. 82

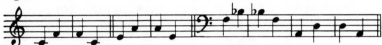

The Augmented Fourth

To read the augmented 4th, a common trick used by good sightsingers is to think a perfect 4th and add a ½ step to it.

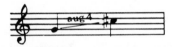

Think and mark as follows:

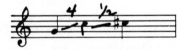

Another way to find the augmented 4th is to think the perfect 5th (see Perfect Fifth) and lower it ½ step.

Example: 4–7 in the major scale ascending, 7–4 descending.

Practice and learn the sound of the augmented 4th.

Exercise: play and sing each interval five times, concentrating on the sound.

Fig. 83

Determine whether each interval is a perfect or an augmented 4th; mark and sing.

Fig. 84

Fifths

Fifths have 2 lines and 1 space or 2 spaces and 1 line between them on the staff.

There are two types of 5ths:

The perfect 5th, with $3\frac{1}{2}$ steps between the notes; and

The diminished 5th, with 3 steps between the notes.

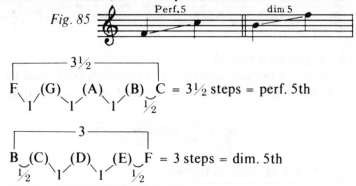

Fig. 85

The Perfect Fifth

In the major scale there are 6 perfect fifths and only 1 diminished fifth, therefore chances are 6 to 1 that any fifth in your music will be a perfect 5th.

The sound of the perfect 5th:

Ascending:

Example: *Twinkle, Twinkle, Little Star*

Twin - kle, twin - kle,   lit - tle   star

Example: 1–5 ascending in the major scale.

Descending:

Example: *For Unto Us a Child Is Born* from Handel's "Messiah."

For   un-to us a child is   born

Practice and learn the sound of perfect 5ths, ascending and descending.

Exercise: play and sing these intervals five times, concentrating on the sound.

Fig. 86

The Diminished Fifth

The sound of the diminished fifth is the same as the augmented fourth.

Sixths

Sixths have a total of 2 lines and 2 spaces between them on the staff.

There are three types of 6ths:

The major 6th, with a distance of 4½ steps between the notes;

The minor 6th, with a distance of 4 steps between the notes; and

The augmented 6th, with a distance of 5 steps between the notes.

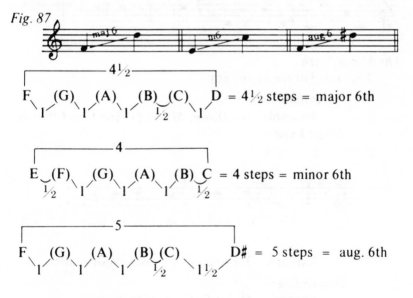

Fig. 87

The Major Sixth

The sound of the major 6th:

Ascending:

Example: *It Came Upon a Midnight Clear*

It came up-on a mid-night clear

Example: 1–6 ascending in the major scale.

Descending:
Example: *Nobody Knows the Trouble I've Seen*

No- bo - dy knows

Example: 6–1 descending in the major scale.
Practice and learn the sound of the major 6th.

Exercise: play and sing each interval five times, concentrating on the sound.

Fig. 88

The Minor Sixth
The sound of the minor 6th:

Ascending:
Example: *Go Down, Moses (When Israel Was in Egypt Land)*

When   Is - rael was in   Eg-ypt land

Example: 3–8 ascending in the major scale.
Descending:
Example: *O, Little Town of Bethlehem*

Beth - le - hem

Example: 8–3 descending in the major scale.
Practice and learn the sound of the minor 6th.

Exercise: play and sing these intervals five times each, concentrating on the sound.

Fig. 89

The Augmented Sixth

For the sound of the augmented sixth, see the Minor Seventh.

Determine whether the intervals below are major or minor 6ths, mark and sing.

Fig. 90

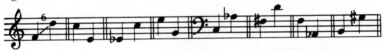

Sevenths

Sevenths have 3 spaces and 2 lines or 2 spaces and 3 lines between them on the staff.

There are two types of 7ths:

The major 7th, with 5½ steps between the notes; and

The minor 7th, with 5 steps between the notes.

Fig. 91

$$\overbrace{\text{C} \quad \text{(D)} \quad \text{(E)} \text{(F)} \quad \text{(G)} \quad \text{(A)} \quad \text{B}}^{5\frac{1}{2}} = 5\frac{1}{2} \text{ steps} = \text{major 7th}$$

C (D) (E) (F) (G) (A) B = 5½ steps = major 7th
1 1 ½ 1 1 1

$$\overbrace{\text{E} \text{(F)} \quad \text{(G)} \quad \text{(A)} \quad \text{(B)} \text{(C)} \quad \text{D}}^{5} = 5 \text{ steps} = \text{minor 7th}$$

E (F) (G) (A) (B) (C) D = 5 steps = minor 7th
½ 1 1 1 ½ 1

$$\overbrace{\text{F} \quad \text{(G)} \quad \text{(A)} \quad \text{(B)} \text{(C)} \quad \text{D♯}}^{5} = 5 \text{ steps} = \text{aug. 6th}$$

F (G) (A) (B) (C) D♯ = 5 steps = aug. 6th
1 1 1 ½ 1½

The minor 7th and augmented 6th are both 5 step intervals and therefore sound exactly the same. If you find it easier to see a minor 7th than an augmented 6th, simply change it in your music:

The Major Seventh

The sound of the major 7th:

Ascending:

Probably the easiest way to find the major 7th is to think the octave higher and subtract ½ step.

Example: 1–7 ascending in the major scale.

Descending:

The major 7th descending can be found by thinking the top note ½ step higher, then thinking down an octave:

Example: 7–1 descending in the major scale.

Practice and learn the sound of the major 7th, ascending and descending.

Exercise: play and sing each of these intervals five times and concentrate on the sound.

Fig. 92

The Minor Seventh

The sound of the minor 7th:

Ascending:

Example: *Silent Night*

Ho - ly Night,   All   is still

Example: 2–8 ascending in the major scale. If you've studied music theory, you'll recognize the minor 7th as the outer notes of a dominant 7th chord.

Descending:

Example: *None But the Lonely Heart*

None but the lone - ly heart

Example: 8–2 descending in the major scale.

Practice and learn the sound of the minor 7th, ascending and descending.

Exercise: play and sing these intervals five times each, concentrating on the sound.

Fig. 93

Determine whether the intervals below are major 7ths, minor 7ths or augmented 6ths, mark and sing:

Fig. 94

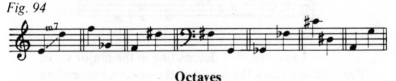

Octaves

Octaves have a total of 3 lines and 3 spaces between them on the staff. In the octaves, both notes have the same sound but are 6 steps apart.

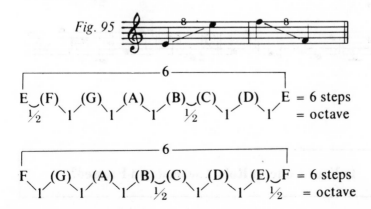

Fig. 95

The sound of the octave:

Ascending:

Example: *Old Folks at Home (Swanee River)*

Swa - nee   Ri - ver

Example: 1–8 ascending in the major scale.
Practice and learn the sound of the octave ascending.

Exercise: play and sing each interval five times, concentrating on the sound.

Fig. 96

· *Descending:*

Example: *Alouette*

A - lou-ette,   A - lou-ette

Example: 8–1 descending in the major scale.
Practice and learn the sound of the octave, descending.

Exercise: play and sing these intervals five times each, concentrating on the sound.

Fig. 97

Is Your Concert Robe Cleaned and Pressed?

Reading Music in Minor Keys

Although there are three forms of the minor scale, six of the eight notes are the same in all forms, and can be learned by the "1,2,3" Method.

Let's look at the natural, harmonic and melodic minor scales. Where are their similarities and differences?

	1	2	3	4	5	6	7	8
Natural minor	C	D	E♭	F	G	A♭	B♭	C
Harmonic minor	C	D	E♭	F	G	A♭	B♮	C
Melodic minor	C	D	E♭	F	G	A♮	B♮	C

Note that 1,2,3,4,5 and 8 are the same in all forms.
Play and sing these notes in the key of C minor:

Fig. 98

Now play and sing the notes for the same degrees in the key of E minor:

Fig. 98a

The notes are different, but the "melody" is the same.

Do these "Play, Sing" exercises five times each, first "thinking" the numbers between the notes, then *without* "thinking" the numbers between the notes.

Exercise 1

Play 1. Sing 1. Sing 3, thinking 2 on the way to 3. Play 3. Sing 1, play 1. Sing 8, play 8.

Exercise 2

Play 1, sing 1. Sing 4, thinking 2 and 3 on the way to 4. Sing 1, play 1. Sing 8, play 8.

Exercise 3

Play 1, sing 1. Sing 5, thinking 2, 3, and 4 on the way to 5.
Sing 1, play 1. Sing 8, play 8.

Try the above "play, sing" exercises in the keys of A
minor, D minor, G minor and E minor.

Sing this C minor melody. Play 1 (C).

Fig. 99

Play 1 (E) and sing this E minor melody.

Fig. 100

Rather than having to learn the three forms of the minor
scale by the "1,2,3" Method, we will simply find the 6th and 7th
degree notes by the Interval Method.

Example: (D minor)

There is no set rule that 1,2,3,4,5 and 8 *must* be found by
the "1,2,3" Method and 6,7 by the Interval Method. For
example, the tonality of 1 is lost when a piece goes through key
changes. In that case, every note may have to be found by the
Interval Method.

Here are two melodies in minor keys to try.

Fig. 101

Fig. 102

You now have the tools of sightsinging. As in mastering any technique, the more time spent at it, the faster you learn.

Using the work you are rehearsing, music you may have around the house, or a book of sightsinging exercises, practice your "1,2,3"s and intervals.

Picture and practice intervals and the sound of "1,2,3" while you are walking the dog, frying an omelette, riding the bus to work, doing the laundry, etc. It can be fun.

Above all, persevere. It will take an investment in time and patience, but think of the dividends at rehearsals and concerts!

Chords

What is a chord? It is a group of three, four or more notes sounded at the same time. In vocal music, of course, we sing these notes consecutively, unless you're like my son, who can whistle and sing in harmony.

Chords have distinctive sounds. Once you have learned to recognize these sounds, you will be able to read three or four consecutive notes as a group.

Triads

There are four kinds of triads (three-note chords): major, minor, diminished and augmented. This is how they are built: any triad is made up of two interlocking intervals of a third. It is built from the bottom up. The lowest note on which 3rds are built is called the root or 1st; the middle note is called the 3rd because it is a third away from the root; the top note is called the 5th because it is a fifth away from the root.

The Major Triad
A major 3rd topped by a minor 3rd. This is a C major triad, abbreviated as C maj. or C.

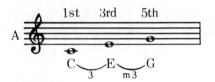

The Minor Triad
A minor 3rd topped by a major 3rd. This is a C minor triad (Cm).

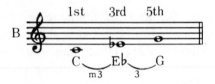

The Diminished Triad
Two minor 3rds. This is a C diminished triad (C dim. or C°).

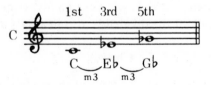

The Augmented Triad
Two major 3rds. This is a C augmented triad (C aug. or C+).

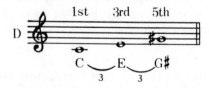

Can you identify these triads?

	1	3	5	Type of Triad
1.	D	F♯	A =	
2.	F	A♭	C =	
3.	B♭	D	F♯ =	
4.	G	B♭	D =	
5.	B	D	F =	
6.	E	G♯	B =	
7.	A	C	E =	
8.	F♯	A	C =	
9.	D♭	F	A =	
10.	C♯	E♯	G♯ =	

Answers at the end of this section.

Build major, minor, diminished and augmented triads on G, B♭, D and F. C is given as a guide.

(*Shortcut:* to build a minor triad, lower the 3rd of the major triad ½ step; to build the diminished triad, lower the 3rd and 5th of the major triad ½ step each; to build the augmented triad, raise the 5th of the major triad ½ step.)

	C			G	B♭	D	F
major triad:	C	E	G				
minor triad:	C	E♭	G				
dim. triad:	C	E♭	G♭				
aug. triad:	C	E	G♯				

In all of the above examples, the root of the triad is the first note you sing (root or fundamental position). There are other arrangements of triads where you sing the 3rd or 5th first. These are called "inversions."

When you sing the 3rd first, the triad is in its *first* inversion.

When you sing the 5th first, the triad is in its *second* inversion.

Whichever the position, the triad is named after its *root* note.

Here are the major, minor, diminished and augmented triads in their three positions:

Major triad:

Minor triad:

Diminished triad:

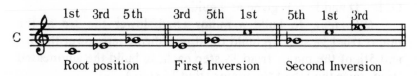

Augmented triad:

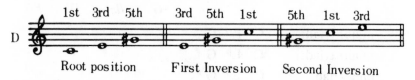

Play and learn to identify the sound of each triad, no matter which position it is in. Have someone else play them for you, if possible.

Determining Whether Three Notes Form a Triad

If you suspect that three consecutive notes you have to learn form a triad, but you're not sure, see if the notes can be arranged in 3rds. If they can, they are the notes of a triad.

For example:

Fig. 103

In the second measure, the notes are F, A and D. Is this a triad? Let's see.

In this arrangement, the intervals are a 3rd and a 4th. Can these notes be arranged to form a triad? There are only two other combinations. Let's try one.

A
\\   / D \\   / F
  \\4/   \\m3/

A 4th and a minor 3rd. No triad yet. One combination left to try.

D
\\   / F \\   / A
  \\m3/   \\3/

Two thirds. Yes! The three notes make up a triad. The root is D. What kind of triad is it? Minor 3rd topped by a major 3rd: by definition, a minor triad. Therefore it is a D minor triad.

Which position is it in? Look at the music. F, the first note you sing is the 3rd of the triad, therefore the triad is in its first inversion.

If you want to impress someone, call it a "D minor triad, first inversion."

Once you have figured out that the three notes form a triad, mark it in your music:

Fig. 103a

Indicate the 1st, 3rd and 5th of the triad and its name.

Exercise: Identify these triads and their inversions. Rearrange if necessary. Which example is *not* a triad?

1.	F	A	D	=
2.	C	E♭	G	=
3.	B	D	G	=
4.	C	F	A♭	=
5.	F	A	C♯	=
6.	B♭	E♭	G	=
7.	F♯	A♯	C♯	=
8.	D	F	A♭	=
9.	G	B	F	=

Answers at the end of this section.

Four-note Chords

Chords may also come in groups of four or more notes, but we do not have to go over four for our purposes.

One of the four-note chords you will come across most often is the triad with its root added an octave higher:

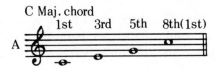

You'll also find the root an octave higher added to minor, diminished and augmented triads:

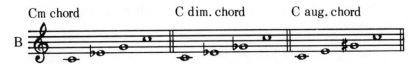

Play and learn the sounds of the four-note chords with octave added.

Another four-note chord that pops up in your vocal line from time to time is the "dominant 7th." It is a major triad topped by a minor 3rd.

Play and learn the sound of the dominant 7th chord.

Some Mysterious Harmonic Terms Explained

Sometimes your conductor may try to explain the harmonic structure of a composition, using the terms "tonic," "subdominant," "dominant" and so forth. This is what they mean.

Each degree of the scale has a technical name:

1. Tonic
2. Supertonic
3. Mediant
4. Subdominant
5. Dominant
6. Supermediant
7. Leading Tone
8. Octave

If you take a degree of the major scale and build a chord on it, that chord will have the same technical name as the degree. The chord built on 1 is the tonic chord. The major chords are traditionally represented by large Roman numerals, the minor and diminished by small Roman numerals.

For example, in the key of C major:

	C	D	E	F	G	A	B	C	D	E	F	Type of
Chord	*1*	*2*	*3*	*4*	*5*	*6*	*7*	*8*	*2*	*3*	*4*	*Chord*
I (tonic)	C		E		G							Major
ii (supertonic)		D		F		A						Minor
iii (mediant)			E		G		B					Minor
IV (subdominant)				F		A		C				Major
V (dominant)					G		B		D			Major
vi (supermediant)						A		C		E		Minor
vii (leading tone)							B		D		F	Diminished

The first column down gives you the Roman numeral and the technical name of the chord.

Across the top are the notes in the key of C and their degree numbers.

Reading left to right from the Chord column under the degree numbers are the notes comprising that chord and its type, i.e., the V or dominant chord in the key of C contains G, B, D and is a major chord.

This table applies to any major key.

Note that the chords built on 1, 4 and 5 are major; chords built on 2, 3 and 6 are minor; the chord built on 7 is diminished.

In minor keys, where there are three different forms, you need remember only this: the tonic and subdominant chords are minor, and the dominant 7th will usually be exactly the same as that of the major key of the same name:

	Tonic	*Subdominant*	*Dominant 7th*
C major	C	F	G7
C minor	Cm	Fm	G7

ANSWERS

Can you identify these triads, Page 107:

1) Major, 2) minor, 3) augmented, 4) minor, 5) diminished, 6) major, 7) minor, 8) diminished, 9) augmented, 10) major.

Identify these triads and their inversions, Page 110:

1) Dm, 1st inversion; 2) Cm, root; 3) G major, 1st inversion; 4) Fm, 2nd inversion; 5) F aug., root; 6) Eb major, 2nd inversion; 7) F# major, root; 8) D dim., root; 9) GBF (not a triad).

To further study the elements of music, may I suggest an outstanding book, "Elementary Harmony" by Robert W. Ottman, published by Prentice-Hall, Inc.

Have You Paid Your Dues?

LOOK IT UP HERE

KEY SIGNATURES

SHARP KEYS	FLAT KEYS

(o = major; ● = minor)

G maj, E m   F maj, Dm

D maj, B m   B♭ maj, G m

A maj, F♯ m   E♭ maj, C m

E maj, C♯ m   A♭ maj, F m

B maj, G♯ m   D♭ maj, B♭ m

F♯ maj, D♯ m   G♭ maj, E♭ m

C♯ maj, A♯ m   C♭ maj, A♭ m

C maj, A m

SYMBOLS

——————◁	*crescendo* (increasing in loudness)
▷——————	*decrescendo* (decreasing in loudness)
◁ ▷	*crescendo, decrescendo* (increasing, then decreasing in loudness)

accents   hold (*fermata*)

staccato (detached)   hold for full value

tie (on same note)

slur (two notes on one word)

,   breath mark

¢   cut time $\left(\frac{2}{2}\right)$

C   common time $\left(\frac{4}{4}\right)$

𝄋   return to sign and repeat

𝄌   to Coda or ending

I°   return to original tempo

♯   sharp (raises note ½ step)

♭   flat (lowers note ½ step)

𝄪   double sharp (raises note two half steps)

♭♭   double flat (lowers note two half steps)

♮   natural (cancels sharps and flats)

Rest Note

= ♪ thirty-second

= ♪ sixteenth

= ♪ eighth

Rest Note

= ♩ quarter

= ♩ half

= 𝅝 whole

(stems up) Soprano
(stems down) Alto

(stems up) Tenor
(stems down) Bass

Written   Sung

appoggiatura
(first note on beat, held long)

acciaccatura
(first note extremely short)

trill

phrase mark:
to be sung in one breath

metronome marking:
60 beats per minute; ♩ = one beat

two voices singing unison

end of section   end of composition

repeat section between dots

10
combined bars of rest

spoken rhythm

Ma-ry had a lit- tle lamb.

MUSICAL TERMS AND ABBREVIATIONS

Italian unless otherwise noted. (G: German; F: French; L: Latin; E: English)

a cappella: unaccompanied voices
accelerando: becoming faster
adagio: slow
ad lib. (L): at will
agitato: agitated
al fine: to the end

alla breve: cut time $\left(\frac{2}{2} \text{ or } \mathꞔ\right)$

allargando: slowing and increasing in volume
allegro: fast
allegretto: moderately fast (between allegro and andante)
allentando: slowing down
all' ottava (8va): an octave higher
ancora: again
andante: moderately slow
anima: spirit
appassionato: intense, with passion
a tempo: in tempo
assai: very
assez (F): enough, rather
attacca: begin next section at once
ausdrucksvoll (G): expressively
aussi (F): also
ben: very
bewegt (G): agitated, somewhat fast
bien (F): very, well
breit (G): broad
brio: vigor
calando: lower in volume, slower in tempo
calmo: calm
calore: warmth
cantabile: in a singing style
cantata: a relatively short dramatic work for chorus and soloists sung without costumes or action
chorale (E): German Protestant hymn tune
coda: end of piece
come prima: as before
con: with
cres., crescendo: increasing loudness
cupo: sombre, dark

D. C., da capo: repeat from the beginning to the end
dal segno: repeat from the sign to the end
dolce: sweet
doppio: double
douce, doux (F): soft, sweet
D. S.: see "dal segno"
e, ed: and
einfach (G): simple, plain
en allant (F): flowing
ernst (G): earnest, serious
esp., espressivo: expressive
et (F): and
etwas (G): somewhat
f; forte: loud
ff; fortissimo: very loud
fff; fortississimo: extremely loud
feierlich (G): solemn
fin (F): end
fine: end
fp; fortepiano: loud followed immediately by soft
frisch (G): brisk, lively
fröhlich (G): glad, joyous
fuoco: fire
gai (F)
gaio } gay, brisk
gesangvoll (G): in a singing style
giocoso: playful
giusto: correct, exact
grave: grave, ponderous, very slow
heimlich (G): mysterious
herzlich (G): heartily
immer (G): always
im zeitmass (G): in the original tempo
innig (G): heartfelt
innigkeit (G): deep emotion
istesso: same
joyeuse, joyeux (F): joyous
klagend (G): mourning
kräftig (G): strong
kurz (G): short, crisp
lamentoso: plaintive
langsam (G): slow
larghetto: slightly faster than largo
large (F): broad

largo: broad
lebhaft (G): lively
legato: smoothly
léger (F): light
leggiero: light
leise (G): soft
lent (F): slow
lento: slow
licht (G): light
lo stesso tempo, l'istesso tempo:
    after change of time signature,
    the value of either the beat or the
    bar remains the same.
lourd (F): grave, ponderous
lustig (G): merry, gay
ma: but
mächtig (G): powerful
maestoso: majestically
maggiore: major
marcato: emphatic
marziale: martially
mass (E): central service of Roman
    Catholic rites
mässig (G): moderate
meno: less
mesto: sad
mezza voce: half voice
mf; mezzoforte: half loud
minore: minor
missa (L): mass
misterioso: mysteriously
mod.; moderato: moderately
modéré (F): moderately
molto: much, very
morendo: dying away
mosso: motion, movement
moto: motion
mp; mezzopiano: medium soft
nicht (G): not
non (F): not
p; piano: soft
pp; pianissimo: very soft
ppp; pppp: extremely soft
pas trop lent (F): not too slow
pesante: heavy
peu à peu (F): little by little
più: more
poco a poco: little by little
pomposo: pompous
portamento: sliding from one note
    to another
presto: very fast
primo (I°): first
quasi: as if, almost

rall.; rallentando: gradually slower
rasch (G): quick
recitativo: reciting
requiem (L): mass for the dead in
    Roman Catholic rites
rinfz.: sudden increase in loudness
rit.; ritardando: gradually slowing
ritenuto: marked reduction in
    tempo
rubato: elasticity of tempo
ruhig (G): quiet
schnell (G): fast
schwer (G): grave, ponderous
segue: next section follows
    immediately
semplice: simple
sempre: always
sf; sfz; sforzando: perform a single
    note with sudden emphasis
sim.; simile: similarly
sostenuto: sustained
sotto voce: with subdued sound
staccato: detached
stark (G): strong
subito: suddenly
tanto: much, so much
tempo: rate of speed of a
    composition
tempo primo: resumption of
    tempo
tendrement (F): tenderly
teneramente: tenderly
tenuto: hold note longer than
    written
tr; trill (E): rapid alternation of a
    note with its upper neighbor
tranquillo: tranquilly
traurig (G): sad
triste (F): sad
tronco: cut off
troppo: too much
tutti: all
unison (E): all performing the
    same melody
un peu (F) ⎱
un poco   ⎰ : a little
vif (F): lively
vite (F): quick
viv.; vivace: lively
voce: voice
zart (G): delicate
zeitmass (G): tempo
ziemlich (G): somewhat, rather
zurückhalten (G): retard

LATIN PRONUNCIATION

(Ecclesiastical Latin of contemporary Roman usage.)

a - f<u>a</u>ther (pater)
e - m<u>e</u>t (<u>e</u>cclesiam)
i - pol<u>i</u>ce (f<u>ili</u>)
o - <u>o</u>r (<u>o</u>mnipotens)
u - m<u>oo</u>d (<u>u</u>num)
y - bab<u>y</u> (lacr<u>y</u>mosa)
ae⎫
oe⎭ g<u>e</u>t (bon<u>ae</u>, c<u>oe</u>li)*

c - (before e, ae, oe, i, y) <u>ch</u>urch (<u>c</u>oeli)
c - (before a, o, u) <u>c</u>at (<u>c</u>onfiteor)
cc - (before e, ae, oe, i, y) ca<u>tch</u> (e<u>cc</u>e) (before other letters) boo<u>kk</u>eeper (o<u>cc</u>asum)
ch - <u>ch</u>aracter (<u>Ch</u>riste)
g - (before e, ae, oe, i, y) <u>g</u>enerous (vir<u>gi</u>ne) (before a, o, u) <u>g</u>one (er<u>g</u>o)
gn - can<u>y</u>on (ma<u>gn</u>ificat)
h - not pronoun<u>ce</u>d, except: (mi<u>h</u>i - mi<u>k</u>i and ni<u>h</u>il - ni<u>k</u>il)
j - <u>y</u>es (<u>J</u>esu)
qu - <u>qu</u>iet (<u>qu</u>i)
r - tri<u>ll</u>ed
s - <u>s</u>ea (<u>s</u>anctus)
s - (between two vowels) <u>z</u>est (mi<u>s</u>erere)
sc - (before e, ae, oe, i, y) <u>sh</u>ow (a<u>sc</u>endit)
sc - (before a, o, u) <u>sc</u>at (<u>sc</u>utum)
ti - (preceded by s, t, x or followed by consonant) pa<u>ti</u>o (hos<u>ti</u>as)
ti - (unaccented, followed by vowel and preceded by any letter other than s, t, or x) Be<u>ts</u>y (gra<u>ti</u>as)
th - <u>Th</u>omas (<u>th</u>eatrum)
v - <u>v</u>ictor (<u>v</u>ivo)
x - e<u>x</u>tra (re<u>x</u>)
x - (in words beginning with "ex" and followed by vowel: e<u>gg</u>s (e<u>x</u>audi)

*also see Diphthongs

xc - (before e, ae, oe, i, y) boo<u>ksh</u>elf (e<u>xc</u>elsis); also e<u>gg</u>shell
xc - (before a, o, u) e<u>xc</u>use (e<u>xc</u>ussorum)
z - la<u>ds</u> (<u>z</u>i<u>z</u>ania)

Diphthongs

In "<u>au</u>", "<u>eu</u>" and "<u>ay</u>", the two vowels form one syllable but both vowels are pronounced, with emphasis on the first:
au (ah'-oo): lauda (lau-da)
eu (eh'-oo): euge (eu-ge)
ay (ah'-ee): Raymundus (Ray-mun-dus)

In "ei", "ii", "eo", "ou", "ai", and in certain cases, "ae" and "oe", each vowel keeps its own sound and is a separate syllable:
ei (eh´-ee): diei (di-e-i)
ii (ee-ee): filii (fi-li-i)
eo (eh´-o as in <u>o</u>r): Deo (De-o)
ou (o´ as in <u>o</u>r-oo): prout (pro-ut)
ai (ah´-ee): ait (a-it)
ae (ah-eh´): Michael (Mi-cha-el)
oe (o-eh´): poema (po-em-a)

Double Consonant

When pronouncing the same consonant doubled, it must be doubled in intensity: e.g. illa (eel-lah)

Greek: Kyrie: Kee-ree-eh
Eleison: Eh-leh-ee-sawn

GERMAN PRONUNCIATION

Vowels are short or long. In general, a vowel is short when followed by a double consonant: Mann, kommen; long when doubled or followed by an h: meer, Bahn.

a (short) - n<u>o</u>t (<u>a</u>ls)
a (long) - star (V<u>a</u>ter)
ä (short) - b<u>e</u>st (Männer)
ä (long) - l<u>a</u>y (sp<u>ä</u>t)
e (short) - r<u>e</u>st (W<u>e</u>lt)
e (long) - pl<u>a</u>y (s<u>e</u>hr)
e (unstressed final)-then (heut<u>e</u>, fall<u>e</u>n)
i (short) - t<u>i</u>n (m<u>i</u>t)
i (long)- s<u>i</u>ng (<u>i</u>hn)
o (short) - <u>o</u>ff (m<u>o</u>rgen)
o (long) - <u>o</u>bey (w<u>o</u>)
ö - turn (round lips for "care" say "core"-h<u>ö</u>ren)
u (short) - p<u>u</u>t (<u>u</u>nd)
u (long) - p<u>oo</u>l (g<u>u</u>t)
ü - round lips for "oo", say "ee" —(f<u>ü</u>nf)
ei - f<u>i</u>ne (ein)
eu - t<u>oy</u> (tr<u>eu</u>)
äu - t<u>oy</u> (H<u>äu</u>sen)
au - <u>ou</u>t (H<u>au</u>s)
ai - m<u>i</u>ght (M<u>ai</u>)
ie - s<u>ee</u>n (hier)

ch - lo<u>ch</u> (Scot) after a, o, u— (na<u>ch</u>)
{ ch - <u>h</u>orse (strong h) after e, i,
  ig - <u>h</u>orse } ä, ö, ü, l, r, n—(i<u>ch</u>, veni<u>g</u>)
ig - also igg or ikk
final d - tea (bal<u>d</u>)
final b - pea (a<u>b</u>)
final g - <u>k</u>eep (ta<u>g</u>)
g - gift (<u>G</u>ott)
j - <u>y</u>ard (<u>j</u>ahr)
l - front of mouth as in "million"
r - as in French, with uvular trill
s - <u>z</u>inc, before a vowel at beg. of word, bet. vowels (<u>s</u>o, Je<u>s</u>us)
s - thi<u>s</u> (da<u>s</u>)
sch - <u>sh</u>ine (<u>sch</u>nell)
sp - <u>sh</u>p } at beg. of word { (<u>sp</u>ät)
st - <u>sh</u>t } { (<u>st</u>ehen)
th - <u>t</u>eam (<u>Th</u>ron)
ti - Be<u>ts</u>y (na<u>ti</u>on)
v - <u>f</u>or (<u>v</u>on)
z - Be<u>ts</u>y (<u>Z</u>ion)
ng - ri<u>ng</u> (si<u>ng</u>en)

ITALIAN PRONUNCIATION

a - f<u>a</u>ther (c<u>a</u>sa)
e - g<u>e</u>t (b<u>e</u>ne)
e - th<u>ey</u> (short y) (m<u>e</u>)
i - mach<u>i</u>ne (l<u>i</u>bri)
o - <u>oh</u> (n<u>o</u>me)
o - <u>or</u> (c<u>o</u>sa)
u - m<u>oo</u>n (<u>u</u>no)
c - (before a, o, u) <u>k</u>ite (<u>c</u>on)
c - (before e or i) <u>ch</u>air (<u>c</u>ena)
ch - (before e or i) <u>ch</u>aracter (<u>ch</u>e)
g - (before a, o, u) <u>g</u>o (va<u>g</u>o)
g - (before e or i) <u>g</u>em (<u>g</u>ente)
gh - <u>g</u>o (fu<u>gh</u>e)
gli - <u>b</u>illion (fi<u>gli</u>)
gn - ca<u>ny</u>on (ba<u>gn</u>o)
h - silent (<u>h</u>a)
qu - <u>q</u>ueen (<u>qu</u>esto)
r - rolled (tongue against gums of upper front teeth) (ca<u>r</u>o)
s - (before p, t, f and at beg. of word (<u>s</u>top (<u>s</u>forzando)
s - (before b, d, g, l, m, n, r, v) and between vowels) mu<u>s</u>ic (a<u>s</u>besto, ca<u>s</u>a)
sc - (before a, o, u) <u>sc</u>ar (pe<u>sc</u>a)
sc - (before e, i) <u>sh</u>op (<u>sc</u>ienza)

sch - <u>sk</u>in (di<u>sch</u>i)
z - be<u>ts</u> (for<u>z</u>a)
z - be<u>ds</u> (<u>z</u>ero)

Diphthongs: each vowel pronounced separately, but if one of them is i or u, they form part of the same syllable; a, e, and o are usually stressed more than i or u.

ie - (pién o)
uo - (uómo)
ua - (guárdia)
io - (giórno)
ei - (miéi)

Double consonants are pronounced much more forcefully than single consonants (almost pronounced twice): bb, cc, gg, pp, tt, vv, mm, ll, ff, nn, zz.

Stress: Most words are stressed on the next to last syllable. (tem´-pi)

Words stressed on the last syllable have a written accent over the last vowel: (città)

FRENCH PRONUNCIATION

(generally pronounced more crisply than English.
All words are accented on the final syllable.)

a - between p**a**rk and h**a**t: (p**a**tte)

$\left.\begin{array}{l}a\\à\end{array}\right\}$ - h**o**t: $\left\{\begin{array}{l}l\underline{a}\\l\underline{à}\end{array}\right.$

â - m**a**rket: (**â**ge)

$\left.\begin{array}{l}ais\\ait\end{array}\right\}$ - l**e**t: $\left\{\begin{array}{l}angl\underline{ais}\\pl\underline{ait}\end{array}\right.$

au - v**o**te, but shorter: (h**au**t)

e - p**u**t: (l**e**, d**e**)

$\left.\begin{array}{l}e\\è\\ê\\est\end{array}\right\}$ - l**e**t: $\left\{\begin{array}{l}b\underline{e}lle\\l\underline{è}ve\\t\underline{ê}te\\\underline{est}\end{array}\right.$

$\left.\begin{array}{l}é\\ed\\er\\es\\et\\ez\end{array}\right\}$ - g**a**te, but shorter: $\left\{\begin{array}{l}all\underline{é}\\pi\underline{ed}\\parl\underline{er}\\l\underline{es}\\\underline{et}\\parl\underline{ez}\end{array}\right.$

eu - t**u**rn: (h**eu**re, n**eu**f)

$\left.\begin{array}{l}i\\î\\y\end{array}\right\}$ - b**ee**: $\left\{\begin{array}{l}f\underline{i}ni\\g\underline{î}t\\myst\underline{è}re\end{array}\right.$

o - n**u**t: (p**o**rte, n**o**te)

ô - v**o**te, but shorter: (h**ô**te)

$\left.\begin{array}{l}oi\\oy\end{array}\right\}$ - s**wa**t: $\left\{\begin{array}{l}v\underline{oi}x\\v\underline{oy}age\end{array}\right.$

os - v**o**te, but shorter: (cl**os**)

ou - m**oo**n: (p**ou**r)

$\left.\begin{array}{l}u\\û\end{array}\right\}$ - round your lips and say "ee": $\left\{\begin{array}{l}f**u**mer\\f**û**t\end{array}\right.$

NASAL SOUNDS*

$\left.\begin{array}{l}am\\an\\em\\en\end{array}\right\}$ - **ah**(n): as in f**a**ther $\left\{\begin{array}{l}j\underline{am}be\\s\underline{an}s\\t\underline{em}ps\\\underline{en}tendre\end{array}\right.$

$\left.\begin{array}{l}aim\\ain\\ein\\im\\in\end{array}\right\}$ - **a**(n): as in b**a**t $\left\{\begin{array}{l}f\underline{aim}\\p\underline{ain}\\h\underline{ein}\\\underline{im}possible\\f\underline{in}\end{array}\right.$

$\left.\begin{array}{l}om\\on\end{array}\right\}$ - **aw**(n): as in s**aw** $\left\{\begin{array}{l}t\underline{om}be\\b\underline{on}\end{array}\right.$

$\left.\begin{array}{l}um\\un\end{array}\right\}$ - **uh**(n): as in **up** $\left\{\begin{array}{l}parf\underline{um}\\br\underline{un}\end{array}\right.$

CONSONANTS

c bef. a,o,u - **c**at (**c**afé, **c**oq, **c**uré)
c bef. e,i,y - **s**et (**c**et, **c**ité, **c**ygne)
ç - **s**ell - (gar**ç**on)
ch - **sh**ow (**ch**anson)
g bef. a,o,u - **g**ap (**g**ai, **g**ond, **g**ué)
g bef. e,i,y - a**z**ure (**g**ens, **g**ît, **g**ypse)
j - a**z**ure (**j**ardin)

h - not pronounced

$\left.\begin{array}{l}qu\\q\end{array}\right\}$ - **c**at: $\left\{\begin{array}{l}\underline{qu}atre\\cin\underline{q}\end{array}\right.$

s between vowels - **z** as in **z**ero; bri**s**er

s in all other cases - **s**it: **s**errer, en**s**emble

All other consonants as in English. Generally, final consonants are not pronounced. Exceptions: c, r, f, l. In the infinitive verb ending "er", the "r" is not pronounced.

Nasal sounds: The nasal "n" sound is an "n" that is started but never completed: the tongue never touches the palate. The nasal "m" sound is exactly the same as the nasal "n" sound. Exceptions: when the letters are in separate syllables; when followed by a vowel; when "n" or "m" is doubled.

EXAMPLES OF INTERVALS

RECOMMENDED RECORDINGS OF POPULAR CHORAL WORKS

Abbreviations: Ang. - Angel; Cap. - Capitol; Col. - Columbia; Dec. - Decca; DG - Deutsche Grammophon; DG ARC - Archiv; Ev. - Everest; Hel - Heliodor; Lon. - London; MCA - MCA None. - Nonesuch; Ody. - Odyssey; Phi. - Phillips; RCA - RCA; Ser. - Seraphim; Turn. - Turnabout; Van. - Vanguard; Vic. - Victrola; West. - Westminster.

Where there is more than one choral work on a record, the coupling is given under the record number.

COMPOSER	WORK	BUDGET	STANDARD
Bach	Christmas Oratorio	Ser. S-6040	DG ARC-2710004
	Easter Oratorio	Vox 8620	Ang. S-36322
	Magnificat in D	Ser. 60001	DG ARC-198197
		(Purcell: Queen Mary)	(Can. 78)
	Mass in B minor	RCA Victrola FVL 2-5715	DG ARC-2710001
	Masses "Lutheran"	None. 73020	DG ARC-2533143/4
	St. John Passion	Ser. S-6036	DG ARC-2710002
	St. Matthew Passion	Van. S-269/72	Ang. S-3599
	Cantata #4 (Christ lag in Todesbanden)	Van. HM 20 (Can. 140)	Ang. S-36014 (V. Williams)
	Can. 78 (Jesu, der du meine Seele)	Van. HM-21E	Ang. S-36354 (Can. 106)
	Can. 80 (Ein feste Burg ist unser Gott.)	Van. S-219 (Can. 104)	DG ARC-198407 (Can. 140)
	Can. 106 (Gottes Zeit ist der aller-beste Zeit)		Ang. S-36354 (Can. 78)
	Can. 140 (Wachet auf!)	Van. HM-20 (Can. 4)	DG ARC-198407 (Can. 80)

COMPOSER	WORK	BUDGET	STANDARD
Beethoven	Missa Solemnis	None. 73002	Ang. 3595
	Mass in C		Ang. S-36775
Berlioz	Te Deum	Ody. 32160206	Phi. 839790
	Requiem	Turn. THS-65017/18	Phi. 6700019
Bernstein	Chichester Psalms		Col. 6792
Bloch	Sacred Service		Col. MS 6221
Brahms	Liebeslieder Waltzes	Ser. S-60033	Col. MS 6236 (op. 52 only)
			RCA LSC 2864 (op. 52 & 65)
	Requiem	Ody. Y 31015	Ang. S-3624
Britten	Ceremony of Carols	Ser. S-60217 (Missa)	Lon. 25271 (Williams: Mass in G)
	War Requiem		Lon. 1255
Bruckner	Te Deum		Ang. S-36615 (Bach: Magnificat)
Fauré	Requiem	None. 71158	Ang. S-35974
Handel	Chandos Anthems	Van. S-227/9 (Nos. 1–11, 3 records)	Argo ZRG-54 (Nos. 6–10)
			Argo 5490 (Nos. 9, 11)
	Dixit Dominus	Van. S-249	Ang. S-36331
	Israel in Egypt	West. 8200	Dec. DXS-7178
	Judas Maccabeus	West. 8201	Desto 6452/4
	Messiah	Ser. S-6056	Phi. SC 71AX300
Haydn	The Creation	Hel. H 25028-2	DG 2707044
	Mass #7 ("In Time of War")	Van. HM28	Ang. S-36417
	Mass #9 ("Nelson")	None. 71173	Argo 5325
	Mass #10 ("Theresa")		Argo 5500
	Mass #12 ("Harmoniemesse")		Argo Z-515

COMPOSER	WORK	BUDGET	STANDARD
Honegger	Roi David (King David)		Lon. STS-15155/6
Mozart	Mass in C ("Coronation")	None. 71041 Vesperae Solennes ("Vespers")	DG 2530356, or Phi. 6707016 [4-rec. set with Requiem, Ave, Exsultate, Kyrie, Mass in C minor ("The Great")]
	Mass in C minor ("The Great")	Turn. 34174	Phi. 6500235
	Requiem	Ser. S-60100	Lon. 1157
	Vesperae Solennes (Vespers)	None. 71041 (Mass in C: "Coronation")	Phi. 6500271 (Ave, Kyrie)
Liszt	Missa Choralis	Turn. 34201	Argo ZRG-760
Orff	Carmina Burana	Ser. 60236	Ang. 36333
	Catulli Carmina	Turn. 4061	DG 2530074
Poulenc	Gloria in G		RCA LSC-2822 (Stravinsky: Sym. of Psalms)
Schubert	Mass in G		MCA 2529 (Mozart: Missa Brevis in B$\flat$)
Stravinsky	Symphony of Psalms		RCA-2822 (Poulenc: Gloria in G)
Vaughan Williams	Dona Nobis Pacem		Ang. S-36972
	Mass in G		Lon. 25271
Verdi	Pezzi Sacri (4) (Four Sacred Pieces) Requiem "Manzoni"	Ser. 6050	Ang. 36125 Lon. 1275
Vivaldi	Gloria	Turn. 34029	Argo Z-505 (Pergolesi: Magnificat)

PUBLICATIONS CONTAINING
RECORD REVIEWS

Published in the United States

Records in Review (annual)—Wyeth Press, Charles Scribner's Sons, New York. (A compilation of High Fidelity Magazine reviews.)

Record and Tape Review (annual)—Scarecrow Press, Metuchen, New Jersey. (Records are rated from "+ +", to "−", poor.

High Fidelity Magazine (monthly)—Billboard Publications, Inc., New York.

Stereo Review (monthly)—Ziff-Davis, New York.

Music Journal (ten times a year)—Sar-Lee Music, Inc., New York.

Consumer Reports (monthly)—Consumers Union of the United States, Inc., Mount Vernon, N.Y.

Notes (monthly)—MLA (Music Library Association), Ann Arbor, Michigan.

The New Listener's Companion and Record Guide, E. H. Haggin (every two years)—Horizon Press, New York.

Published in England

The Stereo Guide (every two years)—The Long Playing Record Library, Cheshire.

Penguin Guide to Bargain Records-–Penguin Books Ltd., Middlesex. (Lists standard-priced as well as bargain records.)

Gramophone Magazine (monthly)—General Gramophone Publications, Ltd., Harrow.

Records and Recordings (monthly)—Hansom Books, London.

Hi-Fi News and Record Review (monthly)—Link House Publications, Ltd., London.

KEY TO PRONUNCIATION OF THE MASS AND REQUIEM IN LATIN

Ah - as in father (amen)

aw - as in awkward, but shorter and with lips rounded (Domine). I use "aw" for want of a closer spelling to the actual sound.

ee - as in police (fili)

eh - as in get (ejus)

oo - as in rule (unum). Caution: the Latin word "lux" is spelled below like the English word "looks", but is pronounced with the long "oo".

ow - as in how (laudate)

The system of syllabification given is the one most frequently used for Latin texts in music.

PRONUNCIATION OF THE MASS IN LATIN

(Portions Most Frequently Sung by Chorus)

Kyrie*
Kee-ree-eh   eh-leh-ee-sawn
Ky -ri -e   e -le -i -son

Kree-steh eh-leh-ee-sawn
Chri -ste e -le -i -son

Kee-ree-eh eh-leh-ee-sawn
Ky -ri -e e -le -i -son

Gloria
Glaw-ree-ah een ek-shehl-sees Deh-aw
Glo -ri -a in ex-cel -sis De -o

Eht een tehr-rah pahks aw-mee-nee-boos baw-neh vaw-loon-
Et in ter -ra pax ho -mi -ni -bus bo -nae vo -lun -
    tah-tees.
    ta -tis.

Low-dah-moos teh. Beh-neh-dee-chee-moos teh. Ah-daw-
Lau -da -mus te. Be -ne -di -ci -mus te. A -do -
    rah-moos teh. Glaw-ree-fee-kah-moos teh. Grah-tsee-
    ra -mus te. Glo -ri -fi -ca -mus te. Gra -ti -
    ahs ah-jee-moos tee-bee praw -ptehr mah-nyahm glaw-
    as a -gi -mus ti -bi pro -pter ma -gnam glo -
    ree-ahm too-ahm.
    ri -am tu -am.

Daw-mee-neh Deh-oos, Rehks cheh-leh-stees, Deh-oos Pah-
Do -mi -ne De -us, Rex coe -le -stis, De -us Pa -
    tehr aw -mnee -paw-tehns. Daw-mee-neh Fee-lee oo-nee-
    ter o -mni -po -tens. Do -mi -ne Fi -li u -ni -
    jeh-nee-teh, Yeh -zoo Kree-steh, Daw-mee-neh Deh-oos,
    ge -ni -te, Je -su Chri -ste, Do -mi -ne De -us,
    ah-nyoos Deh-ee, Fee-lee-oos Pah-trees.
    a -gnus De -i, Fi -li -us Pa -tris.

*Kyrie is in Greek.

Kwee tawl-lees pehk-kah-tah moon-dee, mee-zeh-reh-reh naw-
Qui tol -lis pec -ca -ta mun -di, mi -se -re -re no -
bees, soo-shee-peh deh-preh-kah-tsee-aw-nehm nawb-
bis, su -sci -pe de -pre -ca -ti -o -nem no -
strahm, kwee seh-dehs ahd dehks-teh-rahm Pah-trees.
stram, qui se -des ad dex -te -ram Pa -tris.
Ah-mehn.
A -men.

Credo
Kreh-daw een oo-noom Deh-oom. Pah-trehm aw-mnee-paw-tehn-
Cre -do in u -num De -um. Pa -trem o -mni -po -ten -
tehm, fah -ktaw -rehm cheh-lee eht tehr-rah vee-zee-bee-
tem, fa -cto -rem coe -li et ter -ra, vi -si -bi -
lee-oom aw mnee-oom eht een-vee-zee-bee-lee-oom, eht
li -um o -mni -um et in -vi -si -bi -li -um, et
een oo-noom Daw-mee-noom, Yeh-zoom Kree-stoom, Fee-
in u -num Do -mi -num Je -sum Chri -stum, Fi -
lee-oom Deh-ee oo-nee-jeh-nee-toom. Eht ehks Pah-
li -um De -i u -ni -ge -ni -tum. Et ex Pa -
treh nah-toom ahn-teh aw -mnee-ah seh-koo-lah. Deh-
tre na -tum an -te o -mni -a se -cu -la. De -
oom deh Deh -aw, loo-mehn deh loo-mee-neh, Deh -oom
oom um de De -o, lu -men de lu -mi -ne, De -um
veh-room deh Deh -aw veh-raw. Jeh-nee-toom, nawn
ve -rum de De -o ve -ro. Ge -ni -tum, non
fah -ktoom, kawn-soob -stahn-tsee-ah-lehm Pah -tree,
fa -ctum, con -sub -stan -ti -a -lem Pa -tri,
pehr kwehm aw -mnee-ah fahk-tah soont. Kwee praw-
per quem o -mni -a fac -ta sunt. Qui pro -
ptehr naws aw -mee-nehs eht praw -ptehr naw-strahm sah-
pter nos ho -mi -nes et pro -pter no -stram sa -
loo-tehm deh -shehn-deet deh cheh-lees.
lu -tem de -scen -dit de coe -lis.

Et Incarnatus Est
Eht een-kahr-nah-toos ehst deh Spee-ree-too Sahng-ktaw
Et in -car -na -tus est de Spi -ri -tu San -cto
ehks Mah-ree-ah Veer-jee-neh: eht aw-maw fah -ktoos
ex Ma -ri -a Vir -gi -ne: et ho -mo fa -ctus
ehst.
est.

Crucifixus
Kroo-chee-fee-ksoos eh-tsee-ahm praw naw-bees; soob Pawn-
Cru -ci -fi -xus e -ti -am pro no -bis; sub Pon -
tsee-aw Pee-lah-taw pahs-soos eht sch-pool-toos ehst.
ti -o Pi -la -to pas -sus et se -pul -tus est.

Et Resurrexit
Eht reh-zoor-reh-kseet tehr-tsee-ah dee-eh, seh-koon-doom
Et re -sur -re -xit ter -ti -a di -e, se -cun -dum
    scree-ptoo-rahs. Eht ah-shen-deet een cheh-loom, seh-
    scri -ptu -ras, Et a -scen-dit in coe -lum, se -
    deht ahd dehks-teh-rahm Pah-trees. Eht ee-teh-room
    det ad dex -te -ram Pa -tris. Et i -te -rum
    vehn-too-roos ehst koom glaw-ree-ah yoo-dee-kah-reh
    ven -tu -rus est cum glo -ri -a ju -di -ca -re
    vee-vaws eht mawr-too -aws; koo-yoos reh-nyee nawn eh-
    vi -vos et mor -tu -os; cu -jus re -gni non e -
    reet fee-nees.
    rit fi -nis.

Sanctus
Sahng-ktoos, Sahng-ktoos, Sahng-ktoos, Daw-mee-noos Deh-
San -ctus, San -ctus, San -ctus, Do -mi -nus De -
    oos Sah-bah-awt. Pleh-nee soont cheh-lee eht tehr-rah
    us Sa -ba -oth. Ple -ni sunt coe -li et ter -ra
    glaw-ree-ah too-ah. Aw-zahn-nah een ehk-shehl-sees.
    glo -ri -a tu -a. Ho -san -na in ex -cel -sis.

Agnus Dei
Ah-nyoos Deh-ee, kwee tawl-lees pehk-kah-tah moon-dee,
A -gnus De -i, qui tol -lis pec -ca -ta mun -di,
    mee-zeh-reh-reh naw-bees, daw-nah naw-bees pah-chehm.
    mi -se -re -re no -bis, do -na no -bis pa -cem.

PRONUNCIATION OF THE REQUIEM IN LATIN
(Portions Most Frequently Sung by Chorus)

Requiem
Reh-kwee-ehm eh-tehr-nahm daw-nah eh-ees Daw-mee-neh:
Re -qui -em ae-ter -nam do -na e -is Do -mi -ne:
    eht looks pehr-peh-too-ah loo-cheh-aht eh-ees. Teh
    et lux per -pe -tu -a lu -ce -at e -is. Te
    deh-cheht eem-noos Deh-oos een Tsee-awn eht tee-bee
    de -cet hym-nus De -us in Zi -on et ti -bi
    reh-deh-toor vaw-toom een Yeh-roo-zah-lehm, eggs-
    re -de -tur vo -tum in Je -ru -sa -lem, ex -
    ow-dee aw-rah-tsee-aw-nehm meh-ahm, ahd teh awm-
    au -di o -ra -ti -o -nem me -am, ad te om -
    nees kah-raw veh-nee-eht. Kee-ree-eh eh -leh-ee-
    nis ca -ro ve -ni -et. Ky -ri -e e -le -i -
    sawn, Kree-steh eh -leh-ee-sawn.
    son, Chri -ste e -le -i -son.

Dies Irae
Dee-ehs ee-reh, dee-ehs eel-lah, sawl-veht seh-kloom een
Di -es i -rae, di -es il -la, sol -vet sae-clum in

fah-veel-lah, teh-steh Dah-veed koom See-beel-lah.
fa -vil -la, te -ste Da -vid cum Sy -bil -la.

Kwahn-toos treh-mawr ehst foo-too-roos, kwahn -daw yoo-
Quan -tus tre -mor est fu -tu -rus, quan -do ju -

dehks ehst vehn-too-roos, koon-ktah stree-kteh dees-
dex est ven -tu -rus, cun -cta stri -cte dis -

koos-soo-roos.
cus -su -rus.

Rex Tremendae
Rehks treh-mehn-deh mah-yeh-stah-tees, kwee sahl -vahn-
Rex tre -men -dae ma -je -sta -tis, qui sal -van -

daws sahl-vahs grah-tees, sahl-vah meh, fawns pee-eh-
dos sal -vas gra -tis, sal -va me, fons pi -e -

tah-tees.
ta -tis.

Confutatis
Kawn-foo-tah-tees mah-leh-dee-ktees, flahm-mees ah-kree-
Con -fu -ta -tis ma -le -di -ctis, flam -mis a -cri -

boos ahd-dee-ktees, vaw-kah meh koom beh-neh-dee-ktees.
bus ad -di -ctis, vo -ca me cum be -ne -di -ctis.

Aw-raw soop-plehks eht ahk-klee-nees, kawr kawn-tree-
O -ro sup -plex et ac -cli -nis, cor con -tri -

toom kwah-zee chee-nees, jeh-reh koo-rahm meh-ee fee-nees.
tum qua -si ci -nis, ge -re cu -ram me -i fi -nis,

Lacrymosa
Lah-kree-maw-zah dee-ehs eel-lah kwah reh-soor-jeht ehks
La -cry -mo -sa di -es il -la qua re -sur -get ex

fah-veel-lah yoo-dee-kahn-doos aw-maw reh-oos. Oo-eek
fa -vil -la ju -di -can -dus ho -mo re -us. Hu-ic

ehr-gaw pahr-cheh Deh-oos, pee-eh Yeh-zoo Daw-mee-neh,
er -go par -ce De -us, pi -e Je -su Do -mi -ne,

daw-nah eh-ees reh-kwee-ehm. Ah-mehn.
do -na e -is re -qui -em. A -men.

Offertory (Domine Jesu)
Daw-mee-neh Yeh-zoo Kree-steh, rehks glaw-ree-eh, lee-
Do -mi -ne Je -su Chri -ste, rex glo -ri -ae, li -

beh-rah ah-nee-mahs, awm-nee-oom fee-dehl-ee-oom deh-
be -ra a -ni -mas, om -ni -um fi -del -i -um de -

foon-ktaw-room deh peh-nees een-fehr-nee eht deh praw-
fun -cto -rum de poe-nis in -fer -ni et de pro -

foon-daw lah-koo. Lee-beh-rah eh-ahs deh aw-reh leh-
fun -do la -cu. Li -be -ra e -as de o -re le -

aw-nees, neh ahb-zawr-beh-aht eh-ahs tahr-tah-roos,
o -nis, ne ab -sor -be -at e -as tar -ta -rus,
neh kah-dahnt een awb-skoo-room: sehd see -nyee-fehr
ne ca -dant in ob -scu -rum: sed si -gni -fer
sahng-ktoos Mee-kah-ehl reh-preh-zehn-teht eh-ahs een
san -ctus Mi -cha -el re -prae-sen -tet e -as in
loo-chem sahng-ktahm, kwahm aw-leem Ahb-rah-eh praw-
lu -cem san -ctam, quam o -lim Ab -ra -hae pro -
mee-see-stee eht seh-mee-nee eh-yoos.
mi -si -sti et se -mi -ni e -jus.

Hostias
Aw-stee-ahs eht preh-ches tee-bee, Daw-mee-neh, low-dees
Ho -sti -as et pre -ces ti -bi, Do -mi -ne, lau -dis
awf-fehr-ee-moos. Too soo-shee-peh praw ah-nee-mah-
of -fer -i -mus. Tu su -sci -pe pro a -ni -ma -
boos eel-lees, kwah-room aw-dee-eh meh-maw-ree-ahm
bus il -lis, qua -rum ho -di -e me -mo -ri -am
fah-chee-moos: fahk eh-ahs, Daw-mee-neh, deh mawr-teh
fa -ci -mus: fac e -as, Do -mi -ne, de mor -te
trahns-ee-reh ahd vee-tahm, kwahm aw-leem Ahb-rah-eh
trans -i -re ad vi -tam, quam o -lim Ab -ra -hae
praw-mee-see-stee, eht seh-mee-nee eh-yoos.
pro -mi -si -sti, et se -mi -ni e -jus.

Sanctus
Sahng-ktoos Daw-mee-noos Deh-oos Sah-bah-awt, pleh-nee
San -ctus Do -mi -nus De -us Sa -ba -oth, ple -ni
soont cheh-lee eht tehr-rah glaw-ree-ah too-ah.
sunt coe -li et ter -ra glo -ri -a tu -a.
Aw-zahn-nah een ehk-shehl-sees.
Ho -san -na in ex -cel -sis.

Agnus Dei
Ah-nyoos Deh-ee, kwee tawl-lees pehk-kah-tah moon-dee,
A -gnus De -i, qui tol -lis pec -ca -ta mun -di,
daw-nah eh-ees reh-kwee-ehm (sehm-pee-tehr-nahm).
do -na e -is re -qui -em (sem -pi -ter -nam).

English translations, side by side with the original Latin, are usually included in record albums.

VOCAL RANGES*

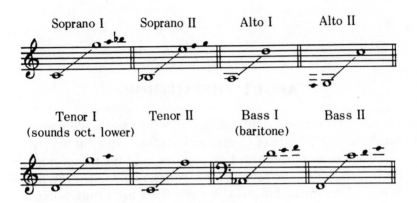

* These are average ranges for non-professional groups. Most people in these groups can sing beyond one or both of the limits shown.

ABOUT THE AUTHOR

Roy C. Bennett is a leading songwriter and a member of the American Society of Composers, Authors and Publishers.

He has written for motion pictures, and the list of popular singers who have recorded his songs reads like a "Who's Who" of the music business. Among them are Frank Sinatra, Perry Como, Andy Williams, Dean Martin, Dinah Shore, Eddy Arnold, Sarah Vaughan, Louis Armstrong, Tony Martin, Cliff Richard, Marty Robbins, the Ames Brothers and many others.

Probably his best known song is the standard "Red Roses for a Blue Lady."

Although popular music has been his vocation, Mr. Bennett's first love has always been the classics, particularly choral music. He started to sing in his high school chorus and has been a member of a chorus ever since.

His musical education includes not only traditional theory and harmony, but also four years of the Schillinger System.

Mr. Bennett is past president of the Great Neck Choral Society in Great Neck, New York.

Index